...DENT'S FIFTH ANNUAL DINNER.
...DEPARTMENT HEADS.
...THE MAYFLOWER.
...EBRUARY. 18,1930.

Schutz
1357

THE
Mayflower

Washington's Second Best Address

BY DIANA L. BAILEY

THE
DONNING COMPANY
PUBLISHERS

Dedication

To my mother Mamie, who gave me this life,
To my husband Kenny, my first love,
To my son Ken Jr., the child of my heart,
To my ever faithful muse, that voice in my heart
who keeps me writing and thinking.
And to the "Heart of the House,"
The men and women of The Mayflower.

The Donning Company Publishers
184 Business Park Drive, Suite 206
Virginia Beach, VA 23462

Steve Mull, General Manager
B. L. Walton Jr., Project Director
Dawn V. Kofroth, Assistant General Manager
Sally Clarke Davis, Editor
Marshall Rouse McClure, Graphic Designer
John Harrell, Imaging Artist
Scott Rule, Senior Marketing Coordinator
Patricia Peterson, Marketing Assistant

Library of Congress Cataloging-in-Publication Data

Bailey, Diana L., 1950–
    The Mayflower : Washington's second best address / by Diana L. Bailey.
        p. cm.
    Includes bibliographical references and index.
    ISBN 1–57864–131–4 (alk. paper)
        1. Mayflower Hotel (Washington, D.C.)—History. I. Title.

TX941.M5 B35 2001
647.95753—dc21

                                                                    2001017166

Printed in the United States of America by Walsworth Publishing Company

Endsheet photo: Guests at "The President's Fifth Annual Dinner to the Department Heads of The Mayflower February 18, 1930" included President Daniel J. O'Brien, center front. The last man pictured on the far left, sitting somewhat apart, is Nicholas Marchitelli, the hotel's second executive chef. Two gentlemen seated in the row second from left would spend their entire careers at the hotel. The first man, leaning forward in glasses, is bandleader Sidney Seidenman. The third gentleman in that row is Corneal J. "C. J." Mack, chief accountant at the time, who would rise to general manager, a position he would hold for more than thirty years. Photo by Schutz.

The Mayflower

Contents

Acknowledgments

The main entrance to 1127 Connecticut Avenue NW swarmed with double-parked limousines and luxury cars the night I arrived at The Mayflower late one rainy Sunday in December 1999 for my first round of meetings and research. The president of the United States or the Israeli prime minister (who was arriving that same weekend for peace talks) could have been in the next car. Yet doorman Frank Agbro greeted me as warmly and efficiently as he would any dignitary, and he would call me by name on every visit thereafter.

Ushered into the beautifully appointed suite reserved for me, I slipped into bed that night daunted by the history and drama into which I was suddenly immersed. I wondered who else had laid their head on these pillows and dared to dream. As surely as the indefinable fragrance of a flower can fill a room, so did I sense the fervent whispers of a thousand voices, each challenging me to tell their story. That challenge would continue to haunt me as, month after month, page after page, interview after interview, aspects of history never before told began to emerge.

In the end, like the oral history told by the descendants of some ancient tribe, it would be The Mayflower family itself—the "heart of the house"—who would graciously, patiently share the myth, magic and mystery of this living edifice. They deserve the credit for the telling of this story; however, any mistakes are undoubtedly my own. General Manager George C. Cook Jr. is the steel-eyed captain of this historic vessel who protects her authenticity with the fierceness of a lord defending his castle, and who envisioned a history to commemorate the Mayflower's seventy-five years as a stage for world events. Crystal Christmas, director of marketing, and Tracy Harris, her assistant, made me welcome, fielded countless calls, set up interviews and extended words of encouragement. Another Mayflower chronicler—night auditor Frank Fleming—would step forward with enormous volumes of information and photos meticulously compiled and annotated. The loan of storeroom manager Willie Gordon's Mayflower albums was both a help and also an honor. Mayflower veteran Jessie Smail, director of convention services, shared personal stories and photos from some of the hotel's most compelling moments. There are so many others to whom I owe so much: Sidney Seidenman Jr. serenaded me with songs and stories from his and his father's musical memories at The Mayflower; Gary Reidinger, director of engineering, led me on a merry chase in quest of the hotel's most priceless art; bell captain Joseph Brackeen, executive chef Norman Wade, executive sous chef Agostino Buggio, bartender Sambonn Lek, housekeeper Emiliana Mercedes, engineer Tony Lamplot, director of human resources Sara Moore, and banquet captain Jimme Curtis trusted me with their Mayflower memories; senior banquet captain Vicente G. Gonzalez's stories could fill his own Mayflower book; housekeepers like Marta Herrera mothered me; Sunil Raikar, director of restaurants, and maitre d'hotel Francois Vezie saw to it that I received "meals on wheels" when I stayed locked in my suite to write; restaurant manager Kostas Tsitoukis and waitress Song Kim served me elegantly in the Café Promenade when I did emerge to eat; Wayne Carney, director of finance, produced priceless archives; and the full Mayflower ship's company at the bell stand, the front desk, the kitchens and restaurants, the wakeup service, hotel message center, the laundry, engineering, and a hundred staff greeted me with the warmth of an old, dear friend.

I especially want to thank Katherine Braxton Walker Butterfield, granddaughter of Mayflower hotel builder Allan E. Walker, for sharing priceless family records and photographs and Mary Katherine Walker, Allan Walker's youngest daughter, who allowed me to witness her first visit ever to The Mayflower, and who also provided intimate glimpses into the visionary entrepreneur who was her father.

Rina Sabatini Conway trusted both me and the mail with rare photos and clippings of her father, Nicholas Sabatini.

The humblest of gratitude goes to Bernie and Lynn Walton, my publishers and friends at both Donning and Hallmark, whose unshakeable belief allowed me to fulfill a lifelong dream.

To Amy Waters Yarsinske—who first trusted me as her editor, believed in me as a writer and loves me as a friend—I owe an enormous debt for her insights and for going down some rabbit holes to ferret out facts that eluded me.

I want to thank my boss and friend, Bill Brown, recently retired from the U.S. Army Corps of Engineers, for his flexibility and support.

Most of all, I want to thank my husband Ken, who tried to keep the world away, and the rest of my family and friends who forgave my single-mindedness as I abandoned them for months to write during those times we would normally spend together.

NATIONAL TRUST
for HISTORIC PRESERVATION

RICHARD MOE
PRESIDENT

Foreword

Some of the most fascinating chapters in our nation's story have been written in the grand hotels that grace many of America's cities. None of these landmark hotels has a greater claim to fame than the subject of this book: "The Mayflower: Washington's Second Best Address."

From its opening day, the Mayflower has been a hub of social life in the nation's capital. Countless election-night victories (and defeats) have been celebrated (and mourned) here, and the Grand Ballroom's tradition of hosting inaugural balls stretches all the way back to Calvin Coolidge's in 1925. Heads of state from Emperor Haile Selassie to Queen Elizabeth II chose the Mayflower as their home-away-from-home on visits to Washington, as did entertainment luminaries from Mary Pickford to Groucho Marx. Charles Lindbergh was honored at a breakfast reception here following his history-making transatlantic flight, and J. Edgar Hoover ate lunch at the hotel almost every day for twenty years.

But the history of the Mayflower is more than a chronicle of famous names and faces. It is also a story of pride and rebirth. A strong, unfaltering commitment to top-quality service has enabled the hotel to keep providing the "rich beauty and intimate refinements" that it first promised its guests more than 75 years ago, and an extensive program of skillful and carefully-researched restoration has revived the luster of important features that had been dimmed by time.

This circa 1930 photograph of The Mayflower's Grand Ballroom, captured in a rare unoccupied moment from its early days, shows the elegant expanse of one of the hotel's renowned public spaces to its fullest advantage. Testaments to The Mayflower's proud "captains," most of the architectural features pictured here have been preserved. Photo by Schutz, courtesy of Frank Fleming.

We are proud that the Renaissance Mayflower is a member of the National Trust's Historic Hotels of America program, which was created to spotlight places such as this—places that provide tangible links with our past, that enhance the quality of life for out-of-town visitors and local residents alike, that offer unique traveling experiences by blending the best of yesterday and today.

Today's Mayflower is everything its original developers imagined and more than they could have dreamed. With a proud past—beautifully documented in this book—and a great future as a vital force in Washington's economy, it is a unique and irreplaceable treasure.

Protecting the Irreplaceable

1785 MASSACHUSETTS AVENUE, NW · WASHINGTON, DC 20036
202.588.6105 · FAX: 202.588.6082 · WWW.NATIONALTRUST.ORG

The Mayflower's stately rooms and vast halls, such as the block-long Promenade, provide fitting accommodations to the world's most important figures.

Introduction

The White House

What is the secret of your subtle sorcery?
"Nobody lives here; men just come and go,"
Said Calvin Coolidge in his vein ironic,
Speaking but half a truth, as he well knew.

Mention your name, and eyes of thousands
    brighten—

You are a symbol, an historic shrine, we know.
Within your walls have lived each president
    since Adams;
Beneath your gracious elms have walked men grave
    with care;
You have known music, laughter, heartbreak
    and travail.

Simple yet stately are your rooms and vast
    your halls;
Glossy your smooth-kept lawns, your flowering
    trees;
Seen thru the mists from yonder Lafayette Square,
You gleam in lovely radiance, so whitely poised.

What man can estimate your worth, intrinsic
    value?
Twenty-two million odd, say realtors, wise figures.
No billionaire could buy for twice that sum in gold.
Yet any poor lad may aspire still to be your master.

Mistress you are of social codes in this, our
    capital.
An invitation to your board must never be declined.
Yet these analyses are incomplete in speaking
    of you.
Fail to define your glowing witchery, your
    magic spell.

We are your children, you possess us all;
E'en as we love, you gently mock our urge
To learn your inmost secrets.
Completely we shall never know you.
Baffling you are and ever-beckoning;
Villa of Glamour, Goal of Cherished Dreams!

Flora G. Orr, The Mayflower's Log

As eclectically fascinating as any *Vanity Fair* or *New Yorker* and of equal literary quality, for decades the *Mayflower's Log* chronicled not only the hotel's clientele and climate but also that of the nation and the world. Flora G. Orr was a regular contributor to the *Log* in the 1940s, although her position, if any, with the hotel is unclear. In its prime, the *Log* featured the writings of statesmen on history, a vicomtesse on fashion, local scholars with reviews on newly released books, even short stories by various authors.

In her own "vein ironic," the author unknowingly foretold the myth, magic and mystique The Mayflower would also attain. Except for one or two phrases, these reverent words, written for the February 1940 *Mayflower's Log* in tribute to the White House, apply equally to The Mayflower's place in history, for in her seventy-five years, she too has become "a symbol, an historic shrine," she too has "known music, laughter, heartbreak and travail." Perhaps Calvin Coolidge—the guest of honor at the first official political function at The Mayflower—uttered the second line ascribed to him as he pondered his decision to decline to run for a second full term in the White House. But his poignant words—"Nobody lives here; men just come and go,"—echo now in The Mayflower's "simple yet stately" transient rooms, where once lived the greatest men and women of the twentieth century.

Like the White House, its neighbor The Mayflower, "Seen thru the mists from yonder Lafayette Square," still gleams "in lovely radiance, so whitely poised." After months of research and interviews, "these analyses are incomplete in speaking of" this Washington monument that rivals even the White House as a place where history continues to be made. Even as the author fell in love with The Mayflower mistress, she failed to completely define the secret of her subtle sorcery, her "glowing witchery," her "magic spell." Ever the discreet lady, The Mayflower still keeps her "inmost secrets." Although "completely we shall never know you," after three-quarters of a century, the "ever-beckoning" Mayflower also endures as a "Villa of Glamour, Goal of Cherished Dreams!" But to know her only a little is to love her forever.

— *Diana L. Bailey*

Streetcar tracks still competed with automobiles on Connecticut Avenue in this 1931 photo of The Mayflower taken through an arched doorway from across the street by renowned D.C. photographer Theodor Horydczak (1890–1971). The photo clearly shows the two wings and the distinct setback of the tower on the right to accommodate the trapezoidal block of land on which the Mayflower was constructed. Frequently referred to as "the artist with the camera," Horydczak would spend days in the study of a particular picture subject until he was "satisfied of the effect to be obtained in the blending of lights and shadows," wrote a Mayflower's Log editor. A native of Russia and a War Department photographer for a number of years, the patient photographer experimented on every clear day for three weeks to obtain what he felt was the right setting of clouds for this artfully framed photo. Photo courtesy of Frank Fleming.

History in the Making
Birth of D.C.'s Grande Dame

*"(T)hey had now no friends to welcome them, nor inns
to entertain or refresh their weather-beaten bodies,
no houses . . . to repair to, to seek for succor."*

—Of Plimouth Plantation, *the journal of*
William Bradford, governor of Plymouth Colony

Washington at the dawn of the twentieth century was a fledgling capital city in a near-new nation. One man with a vision would build an edifice that today stands rivaled only by older landmarks in ancient cities. This man and his name would be forgotten, but his dream—The Mayflower—endures as a stage for world events as alluring in this new century as she was in the last.

In the early 1900s, with the exception of such hotels as the Willard, rooming houses were still the primary public accommodations for travelers to Washington, D.C. Even political and business leaders were relegated to private mansions for visits, meetings and affairs of state. Wrote prominent Washington architect Robert F. Beresford of that time, "During the past ten years the population of Washington has increased from 380,000 to approximately 500,000. This increase, due to the augmented importance of the nation in international affairs and of the Nation's Capital in domestic affairs, the constant flow of foreign representatives and visitors, and among our own countrymen the habit of travel to the nation's shrine, has been accompanied by a marked expansion in the business area of the city."

To serve these important guests, builder Allan E. Walker, a third generation Washingtonian, set into motion his dream: an elegant hotel in the tradition of the grand hotels of Europe's gilded age. During the boom following World War I, Walker, a prominent businessman and city booster, had already developed the prosperous Brookland area of the city as well as large areas of northwest Washington. The location he chose—a former convent and Catholic school for girls, where weary souls had found refuge for decades—was just four blocks from the White House, a site he though would be the perfect location to erect a facility that he intended would bear his name. His choice would prove paradoxical for, while ultimately this Mecca would become the crossroads for world events, unforeseen forces of nature would prove Walker's demise.

The Order of the Visitation of Holy Mary (VHM) was founded in 1610 in southeastern France by Saint Jane de Chantal and Saint Francis de Sales (for whom the cross street was named where The Mayflower now stands). Heeding a call to serve in Washington, D.C., in 1877 members of the order eventually built the Academy of the Visitation for Young Ladies in a section of the city that was then considered "country," in keeping with the founders' vision of a monastic order "nurtured in a life of interior prayer."

By the turn of the century, the nation's capital was already one of the nerve centers of the world. Its rapid spread soon swallowed up surrounding land, including the Order's once peaceful place. Lower Connecticut Avenue had become an elegant thoroughfare lined with embassies, expensive apartment houses and fine shops.

> ## 1927
> The Honorable Vincent Massey, Minister from Canada, and his wife set up their domicile at The Mayflower. Massey is the first diplomatic representative ever sent by his country to Washington.

Wrote Beresford, "With these inevitable changes Connecticut Avenue, formerly the fashionable residential street of the Capital, has become a business thoroughfare of high-class shops and has acquired the title, 'The Fifth Avenue of Washington.'"

Surrounded now by the outside world, convent officials sold the land and moved to another then-isolated area, described by Sister Mada-Anne Gell, VHM, current archivist of Georgetown Visitation Convent, as "way out in Bethesda, Maryland," an area that would eventually become the center of the National Institutes of Health. By 1922, the original Academy of the Visitation for Young Ladies on Connecticut Avenue had been razed, and Allan Walker purchased a major portion of the property.

During the late 1800s, a lack of control over the rapid, haphazard growth of Washington, D.C., saw an erosion of Pierre Charles L'Enfant's vision of a planned city. But a meeting of the American Institute of Architects convened in Washington in 1900—the centennial of the establishment

As described in a 1925 article by The Mayflower architect Robert F. Beresford in the publication Through the Ages, ". . . a circle of convent walls sheltered a garden close where laughing children trooped in and out while stately sisters strolled, reverently murmuring their prayers or telling their rosaries." The convent walls were those of the Academy of the Visitation for Young Ladies built in 1877 and pictured here some time after 1908. The horse-drawn van in the foreground brought deliveries from the Logemann & Leyking Bakery, which operated from 1908 to 1930 at 1751 L Street, just a block away. The Visitation's facility was huge, according to Sister Mada-Anne Gell, VHM, archivist of Georgetown Visitation Convent. "It was just a beautiful building and very large, because it was where the nuns lived, and it was a boarding and day school." By the early 1900s, Washington's rapid growth had swallowed up the land surrounding the convent and threatened to disrupt the founders' vision of a monastic order "nurtured in a life of interior prayer." School enrollment had also declined from competition by more up-to-date Catholic schools in Washington. By 1919 the school had closed, and convent officials sold the land and moved to Bethesda, Maryland. Photo courtesy of Historical Society of Washington, D.C.

STRONG SECURITY

A direct closed first and four-fold mortgage on: (1) Corner fee of approximately an acre and a half (153.89'x455.73'x140') (2) Fireproof eleven-story hotel building with three connecting eight-story apartment structures containing a majority of furnished suites (3) Furnishings and equipment (4) Net annual earnings which are estimated by the borrower to be over three and three-quarters times heaviest annual interest charge.

View Surrounding Hotel Site

STRATEGIC LOCATION

The property is located in residential and governmental Washington within a few blocks of the White House. The hotel and apartments will be convenient for the expanding housing needs of both private and official Washington, the hotel demands of thousands of frequent business and recreational visitors and available for the many social and diplomatic functions of the Capital City. The hotel and apartment needs at Washington are always constant because governmental business never ceases.

DISTINCTIVE BUILDING

The construction will be of reinforced concrete—sound-proof walls—with limestone and rough-faced brick exterior. It will contain a promenade over 400 feet long, commodious lounge with pipe organ, mezzanine entirely surrounding the lobby and spacious ballroom. Almost three acres of space will be devoted to public use. The first two floors will contain a palatial dining salon, café, grill room, palm court (40'x50'), restaurant and private banquet and writing rooms.

$4,200,000
Issue to be Secured by First Mortgage on

Walker Hotel and Apartments
(To be Erected at S. E. Corner Connecticut Ave. and De Sales St., Washington, D. C.)

7%
First Mortgage
Real Estate
Gold Bonds
7%

Nation's Capitol

EXPERIENCED PERSONNEL

The owners and operators of the building will be Walker Hotel Corporation of which Mr. Allan E. Walker is President, William L. Browning, Secretary and Treasurer. Mr. Walker and associates also are successful operators of other Washington property. Robert F. Beresford designed the building and will be assisted in superintending its construction by Mr. F. F. Gillen, former Superintendent of Public Buildings and Grounds, D. C., who also supervised the erection of Lincoln Memorial, Arlington Amphitheatre and other large government buildings. Warren and Wetmore of New York City are the consulting architects.

Aeroplane View of Washington

Maturities 2 to 12 years. Bonds to be dated June 15, 1922. Callable at option of owner at 103 and accrued interest. Guarantors: Allan E. Walker and William L. Browning. Trustee: Chicago Title & Trust Co.

Interest payable June 15 and Dec. 15 at offices of American Bond & Mortgage Co., Inc. Normal Federal Income Tax up to 4% paid by Borrower when claimed.

Interest Payable at Offices of American Bond & Mortgage Company *(Incorporated)*

MATURITIES

$40,000 due June 15, 1924		$90,000 due June 15, 1929	
90,000 " Dec. 15, 1924		90,000 " Dec. 15, 1929	
90,000 " June 15, 1925		90,000 " June 15, 1930	
90,000 " Dec. 15, 1925		90,000 " Dec. 15, 1930	
90,000 " June 15, 1926		90,000 " June 15, 1931	
90,000 " Dec. 15, 1926		90,000 " Dec. 15, 1931	
90,000 " June 15, 1927		90,000 " June 15, 1932	
90,000 " Dec. 15, 1927		90,000 " Dec. 15, 1932	
90,000 " June 15, 1928		90,000 " June 15, 1933	
90,000 " Dec. 15, 1928		90,000 " Dec. 15, 1933	
		$2,450,000 due June 15, 1934	

Bonds in denominations of $100, $500, and $1,000. $100 bonds available only in maturities of June 15, 1928 and June 15, 1934.

This center spread from a 1922 investment brochure published by the American Bond & Mortgage Company describes the "Walker Hotel and Apartments" as a "Fireproof eleven-story hotel building with three connecting eight-story apartment structures." Features would include "a promenade over 400 feet long, commodious lounge with pipe organ, mezzanine entirely surrounding the lobby and spacious ballroom," as well as "a palatial dining salon, café, grill room, palm court (40' x 50'), restaurant and private banquet and writing rooms." The brochure also states specifically that "Robert F. Beresford designed the building," not Warren & Wetmore, the firm that would later be credited with design. Instead Warren & Wetmore were listed as "consulting architects." Note here that the rendering showed the apartment annex three floors shorter than the hotel itself. Only a two-floor difference in the height existed after construction and much of the architectural detailing on the outside was modified as well.

of the federal city—set standards that marked a return to classic architecture. States Christopher Weeks in his *Guide to the Architecture of Washington, D.C.*, ". . . some of the finest buildings in Washington date from the early decades of this century quite simply because the best architects in the country designed them." While The Mayflower is listed as one of those "finest buildings," who deserves credit for this accomplishment is debatable.

Contemporary architectural publications and references almost universally credit the New York firm of Whitney Warren and Charles Wetmore as The Mayflower's architects of record. However, earlier records suggest otherwise. A 1922 brochure published by the American Bond & Mortgage Company, showcases the "Walker Hotel and Apartments" as its premier investment opportunity. It states: "Robert F. Beresford designed the building and will be assisted in superintending its construction by Mr. F. F. Gillen, former Superintendent of Construction for 23 years for the Board of Public Buildings and Grounds, D. C., who also supervised the erection of Lincoln Memorial, Arlington Amphitheatre and other large government build-

ings. Warren & Wetmore of New York City are the consulting architects." In building plans preserved under Plexiglas by Anton "Tony" Lamplot, a senior member of The Mayflower's Engineering Department, Beresford, Warren & Wetmore get equal billing as "associate architects." An article in the September 1940 *Mayflower's Log* also credits Beresford as the "original architect of The Mayflower, who has likewise participated in every structural change and decorative revision since the founding of the hotel." Finally, in "Through the Ages," an article he authored which was published at the time of the hotel's opening, Beresford wrote, "The associate architects were Robert F. Beresford and Warren & Wetmore."

Beresford certainly had the credentials. After having served on the staff of the Supervising Architect of the Treasury and in the office of the Superintendent of the Capitol, he had begun his private practice in Washington in 1925. According to a paper written by Robert E. Oshel, Ph.D., for a December 3, 1994, meeting of the Latrobe Chapter of the Society of Architectural Historians, Beresford would later design the Tower Building at 14th

This early close-up view of the hotel, taken at the corner of De Sales Street (left) and Connecticut Avenue, highlights the terra-cotta trim and quoins, urns and carriage lights that added lovely details to the hotel when built. Photo by Reni Newsphoto Service, courtesy of Frank Fleming.

and K Streets as well as "hundreds of colonial style homes in the Washington area." Beresford also served a term as president of the Washington Chapter of the American Institute of Architects. Considering Allan Walker's standing as president of his highly successful development company and Beresford's position as head of a small but prominent D.C. architectural firm, they were most likely not only contemporaries and acquaintances, but also allies in Washington's development.

Undoubtedly determined that his hotel must rival those grande dames of Europe and other parts of America, Walker apparently also turned to the partnership of Whitney Warren and Charles Wetmore to consult on design. Most renowned for their work on New York's Grand Central Terminal, Warren & Wetmore had become the architects of choice for the nation's most luxurious hotels, including New York's Vanderbilt, the Biltmore and Commodore Hotels built adjacent to Grand Central Terminal; the Ritz Carltons in both New York and Atlantic City; as well as the Broadmoor in Colorado Springs. In any case, the collaboration of Warren, Wetmore and Beresford would produce an architectural marvel whose beauty would transcend time.

Two challenges in particular set limits to design. The main avenues such as Connecticut that radiate from Washington's famous circles create odd building lots. The lot from which The Mayflower would rise is a trapezoid, the corner of De Sales and Connecticut jutting into almost a pie shape. Also, then

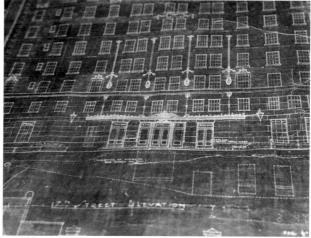

In these plans dated October 6, 1922, the name of the hotel is still listed as "Hotel Walker." The second photo at right shows the 17th Street entrance at the opposite end of the Promenade. Notice the architectural friezes planned for the face of the hotel. Contemporary references give sole credit for The Mayflower's design to Warren & Wetmore; however both Robert F. Beresford and Warren & Wetmore get equal billing as "associate architects" on these original drawings. Photos by the author.

as now, Washington is a horizontal city, constrained by building heights set in 1910 to ensure that commercial construction would not overshadow federal monuments.

Architectural historians refer to The Mayflower's design as neoclassical and, more precisely, Beaux Art. It is the epitome of architectural eclecticism, an elegant, tasteful confection blending the best of Roman, Renaissance and Baroque styles. While records conflict as to who was principal designer, certainly Warren's training at the Ecole des Beaux Art in Paris and Wetmore's Harvard education and New York architectural apprenticeship, influenced the creation of "a dynamic solution to the design problems posed by its trapezoidal lot," according to the hotel's historic landmark designation. "The dramatic angle of the west façade, with its two curved towers, combined with the imposing yet carefully proportioned bulk of the hotel's north wing along De Sales Street, uses the site to generate a spectacular grand perspective up Connecticut Avenue." When completed, the perimeter of the building would measure nearly a quarter of a mile. The Connecticut Avenue frontage would rise eleven stories, while the height of the remainder of the building, governed by the city's zoning restrictions, would reach only nine. (Renovations in the 1980s would add two floors to these sections as well.)

Ground was broken in July 1922 but almost immediately trouble plagued construction. The contractor, Longacre Engineering and Construction, ran into an underground creek, Slash Run, a small tributary of nearby Rock Creek, and was forced to dig down to bedrock to reach stable footing for the hotel's foundation. Slash Run was one of several waterways that had been previously relegated to underground sewers once their waters grew polluted or builders coveted the land through which they flowed.

The stream was not the only discovery. Beresford, in an article published just months after The Mayflower opened, described "an ancient swamp, buried under the debris of the centuries:"

Interest in this discovery was heightened when there were unearthed 30 feet below ground a number of huge stump remains of prehistoric trees, some of which were more than 8 feet in

Mayflower *mania was still sweeping the nation after the tercentennial celebration of her landing in Plymouth. Once Allan Walker lost controlling interest of both the hotel and its name, financiers determined the name* Mayflower *suited their flagship hotel. This replica of the* Mayflower *is the same one that has been on permanent display in the lobby since opening day and stands today behind the concierge desk. A 1980 appraisal lists it as "a large decorative non-scale model custom made for the Mayflower Hotel, ca. 1925; hull and rigging restored in 1955 by William Travis Gibb, M.D., Washington, D.C." valued at $1,200 at the time. Photo by Bob Jackson, courtesy of Frank Fleming.*

diameter and of an age estimated by scientists to be at least 30,000 years. So were brought to view, in the palm of time, the structural materials of an ancient era. But they were of a day that is done. The wood, white when brought to the surface, on exposure to the air turned brown and promptly succumbed to the forces of decay.

The two geological hurdles delayed progress for months and incurred enormous cost overruns, eventually pushing construction to $11 million, an unheard of amount for the time. Sadly, in September 1924, just months before the "Hotel Walker" was to open, Walker was forced to turn over controlling interest to C. C. Mitchell, an officer of the American Bond & Mortgage Company, a major financial backer of the project. Controlling interest apparently included the hotel's naming.

As with the lingering bicentennial celebrations of American independence that stirred patriotism and renewed a ground swell of interest in U.S. history in 1976, Washington and the nation had yet to come down from the high that swept the nation during the tercentennial celebration of the *Mayflower* landing in 1620. Even after the 1920 anniversary, *Mayflower* mania continued. The theme became the absolute symbol of everything elegant and noble. What better name for this flagship hotel than "The Mayflower," the image of perseverance and permanence.

A replica of the *Mayflower* vessel was commissioned, the same replica that has been on permanent display in the lobby since opening day and stands proudly today behind the concierge desk. The new owners pushed on, ordering plush carpeting, regal fixtures and stately furniture to

1930
Boxer Gene Tunney is guest speaker at the Georgetown University banquet held at The Mayflower May 8th.

Even for 1925 monetary standards, rooms that offered not only a private bath but also "circulating ice water" were surely a bargain starting at only $5, as shown in The Mayflower's first advertising brochure. The brochure also offered another now-rare bargain: "A fixed policy of the hotel, and one which is receiving favorable comment throughout the nation, is that no advance in rates is made at the time of great celebrations or national observances in Washington, such, for instance, as Presidential Inaugurations."

appoint their new flagship. Guests would eat from gold-rimmed dishes and crystal bearing a silhouette of the vessel *Mayflower*, and dance in a grand ballroom surrounded by marble pillars under a vaulted ceiling decorated in glittering 23-karat gold leaf, more gold than in any Washington building except the Library of Congress.

Assured that The Mayflower was ready to meet every need of her overnight guests and residents, it was time to throw out the welcome mat and greet the world in her soon-to-be-celebrated public spaces. An official opening was set for February 18, 1925. However, another more "private" celebration came first. On February 17, seven hundred fifty special guests, those who had designed, constructed and equipped the hotel, as well as political, social and financial leaders attended The Mayflower's first com-

ing-out party at which the hotel itself was the debutante.

On opening day February 18, 1925, "The temperature hovered near a comfortable 60 in the National Capital . . . as powerful floodlights outlined a flag-bedecked hostelry whose opening had already attracted widespread interest. Throughout the day, hundreds of Washingtonians gathered in the neighborhood for a first glimpse of The Mayflower," stated an anniversary issue of the *Log* fifteen years later. According to Judith R. Cohen, author of a 1987 history of the hotel, fifteen hundred guests, whose invitations bore Pilgrim tercentenary one-cent U.S. postage stamps specially reissued for the occasion, thronged to the first public Mayflower function in the Grand Ballroom, the annual banquet of the Washington Chamber of Commerce. Popular bandleader Vincent Lopez led his orchestra in the Presidential Dining Room where celebrated maitre d'hotel Fred Wiesinger—once a fixture at the dining room of the old Shoreham Hotel—greeted old friends. As souvenirs of

This first Mayflower advertisement, which ran before the hotel opened in 1925, was certainly optimistic. Prospective tenants must have been lining up in numbers, for advertisers felt confident enough to declare The Mayflower the "Permanent home of Statesmen, Diplomats and Society." Managers were equally confident of opening time. While builder Allan Walker was turning over controlling interest, the new management was already accepting advance reservations for "Washington's newest and finest hotel" opening "after the middle of February."

Hotel staff stand at the ready in the flower bedecked lobby on opening day, February 18, 1925. Photo courtesy of Frank Fleming.

the history-making event, guests were given "Pilgrim half-dollars, which had been issued in 1920 to commemorate the three hundredth anniversary of the landing of the ship *Mayflower* at Plymouth Rock," wrote Cohen.

The next day, February 19, The Mayflower's first full day of business, "a brilliant sun showered its rays upon the cream colored façade . . . as a carefully recruited staff gave evidence that a truly great hostelry was 'open for business,'" according to one account of the time. Major Henry Rowan Lemly, U.S. Army (retired), became the first guest to sign the register. A scholar and respected author as well as a soldier, Lemly had served in overseas assignments in such far-flung cities as Bogota, Colombia, and San Juan, Puerto Rico, from where he wrote compelling accounts on both history and culture that were published in the late 1880s in such publications as *Harper's* and *The Century*.

One of America's largest hotels when it opened, The Mayflower featured more than 1,000 guest rooms, including 112 one-to-nine room apartments. Wrote Beresford:

As a public hostelry The Mayflower is unquestionably unique in one important respect: the luxuriousness of its appointments . . . The rooms and apartments are not "furnished" with "sets";

1931

His Imperial Highness Prince Takamatsu of Japan and Princess Takamatsu attend a Mayflower state reception April 16th.

no two alike, they are appointed with carefully chosen individual pieces, each having its special interest for grace, beauty and refinement, and in careful harmony with the color schemes of the rooms. These, with their drapes and bed-hangings of silk, many with over drapes of satin damask; bed lamps and boudoir lights with silken shades; objects of art in harmonious colorings; original watercolors, mezzotints and etchings on the walls—have all the distinction and charm of private dwellings. . . . In the more than 100 semi-housekeeping suites including living-room 26 feet long, dining-room, bedrooms and baths, perfectly equipped kitchens with individual ice machines, electric ranges and complete service of china, linen and silver, is given every facility for the comfort and convenience of permanent guests. An unusual feature of these apartments are the open fireplaces designed for a real open fire and faced with Italian Botticino marble.

In addition to the room appointments, The Mayflower also provided a unique array of services, including maid, laundry and catering facilities, barber and beauty shops, a house doctor and a small emergency hospital, not to mention the city's first "multiple switchboard" telephone system. It also boasted one other feature in its public rooms that set it apart from all others: The Mayflower was the first hotel in Washington to offer "air-cooling." It was no wonder The Mayflower would quickly eclipse such Washington hotels as the smaller Willard built twenty-five years earlier and lacking The Mayflower's modern appointments and grand public spaces.

In a bitter footnote to the successful launching, Allan Elliott Walker died suddenly of a heart attack on May 14, 1925, just three months after The Mayflower's grand opening. Perhaps the financial strains or the challenges of maintaining the high standards he had set for her proved too much. Or perhaps his heart and spirit were finally broken at the loss of what was to have been his legacy to the Nation's Capital. One can only hope that, before his death, he knew at least to some degree the level of achievement his dream would realize.

Color highlights the lobby appointments in the original of this postcard (above) mailed April 7, 1930, to Mrs. A. Stuart in Brooklyn, New York. The description on the back reads, "The Mayflower is a hotel in keeping with the grandeur and beauty of the Nation's Capital. It is located on Connecticut Avenue, the 'Fifth Avenue' of Washington, center of smart shops, near Government Departments, Embassies, and on the threshold of the exclusive residential section. Its Promenade, Presidential Room, Palm Court, Ball Room and Garden are considered among the most beautiful rooms in the United States." The inset postcard is a contemporary artist's rendering of the lobby today, a model of historic restoration and preservation. Postcards courtesy of the author.

From the beginning, The Mayflower's greatest asset has always been its grand public spaces, shown here as they were in 1925.

1933

Will Rogers conducts a mock Senate session to a distinguished audience of senators May 21st that is broadcast over a nation-wide hookup by the National Broadcasting Company.

Suites like these cost about $18 per day in 1925. As Mayflower designer Beresford wrote of the rooms: "no two alike, they are appointed with carefully chosen individual pieces, each having its special interest for grace, beauty and refinement, and in careful harmony with the color schemes of the rooms. [W]ith their drapes and . . . boudoir lights with silken shades; objects of art in harmonious colorings; original watercolors, mezzotints and etchings on the walls—[they] have all the distinction and charm of private dwellings." "Modern" telephones provided the latest in communication through the hotel's renowned switchboard. The first Mayflower brochure boasted, "Oscillating electric fans on brass wall plaques freshen the air, while wide French windows and double French doors insure active ventilation." Note that in the top picture, the back wall is at an angle, indicating its location at the front of the hotel in one of the curved towers. Top photo by Underwood & Underwood, bottom photo by Joe Tenschert, of Tenschert Photo Company; both courtesy of Frank Fleming.

Hotel and
Apartments

The Mayflower
Washington, D.C.

Telephone Main 9800

Cable Mayflower

Executive Offices

January 14, 1926.

Mr. Stephen S. Jewett,
Masonic Temple,
Laconia, New Hampshire.

My dear Mr. Jewett:

Your attention, I feel sure, has previously been
called to The Mayflower, frequently termed the most beautiful
hotel in America. The management, however, wishes again to re-
mind you of the appeal which this outstanding institution makes
to a discriminating traveling public and to express the hope
that, if you have not already done so, you will honor us with
your patronage in the near future.

The Mayflower embodies the latest and most pro-
gressive ideas in hotel construction, equipment and management,
and as one of the largest and most beautiful hotels in this
country it merits the attention of those travelers who are content with nothing less than the best. Because of the distinction of its atmosphere, the perfection of its service and the
very decided excellence of its cuisine, this hotel has become
the gathering place of that cosmopolitan mixture of statesmen,
diplomats and leaders of the financial and social worlds which
renders Washington unique among American cities.

The Mayflower has the additional convenience of a
central location, being not only within easy walking distance of
the theatre and business district, but also at the threshold of
the exclusive downtown residential section.

As these are qualifications which will undoubtedly
appeal, we feel sure that you will find The Mayflower in every
way adequate to your needs, and hope that you will make it your
headquarters whenever you are in the city.

Sincerely yours,

President.

H.L.M.-mb

Less than one year after opening, The Mayflower had already "become the gathering place of that cosmopolitan mixture of statesmen, diplomats and leaders of the financial and social worlds which renders Washington unique among American cities," according to this January 14, 1926, letter to Mr. Stephen S. Jewett, Masonic Temple, Laconia, New Hampshire, signed by Henry L. Merry, The Mayflower's first president and general manager who served from 1925 to 1927. Courtesy of the author.

Amenities that set The Mayflower apart to both visitors and permanent residents included barber and beauty shops, unparalleled banquet services, an apothecary, a house doctor and a small emergency hospital, not to mention the city's first "multiple switchboard" telephone system. The hotel quickly eclipsed such Washington hotels as the smaller Willard built twenty-five years earlier and lacking the Mayflower's modern appointments and grand public spaces. Barber shop and banquet service photos courtesy of Frank Fleming.

DIRECTORY OF MAYFLOWER SERVICES

Art Gallery
OFF MAIN ENTRANCE LOBBY

The Gordon Dunthorne Galleries always offer interesting exhibitions

Barber Shop
BELOW LOBBY AT MAIN ENTRANCE

Telephone: Extension 55

Perfectly appointed for tonsorial shoe shining and manicure service in its own quarters or guest rooms.

Bus Service
STARTER AT MAIN ENTRANCE LOBBY

Telephone: Extension 49

Sightseeing, Automobile and Taxi service, provided by the Mayflower Taxicab and Sightseeing Company, Inc.

Checking Rooms
OFF MAIN LOBBY NEAR FRONT DESK, AND IN THE PROMENADE NEAR ELEVATOR LOBBY

Confectionery
NEWS STAND TO RIGHT OF CONNECTICUT AVENUE ENTRANCE

Telephone: Extension 46

Druggist
TSCHIFFELY BROS., 1203 CONNECTICUT AVENUE

Telephone: Extension 84

Direct telephone service from The Mayflower.

Flowers
OFF MAIN ENTRANCE LOBBY

Telephone: Extensions 10 or 14

The Mayflower Florist provides the finest cut flowers and potted plants.

Garage
Telephone: Metropolitan 5000

Within a few steps of the hotel, a private fireproof garage is equipped for every kind of service by expert mechanics.

Gifts
OFF MAIN LOBBY ON DE SALES STREET SIDE

Telephone: Extension 71

The Ship's Bell offers a variety of souvenirs, trinkets, novelties and articles for home decoration.

Gowns
MEZZANINE FLOOR

Telephone: Extension 58

The Pearle Cutting Dress Shop expressing sophistication in clothes for sport, afternoon and evening.

Hairdresser and Manicurist
MEZZANINE FLOOR

Telephone: Extension 38

All services performed by experts under direction of Pearle Cutting. Toilet articles and preparations.

House Physician
Telephone: Extension 277

OFFICE—SUITE 277
DR. F. A. HORNADAY

Information
Telephone: Extension 78

Front Office Information Bureau supplies courteous attention to all inquiries.

Laundry
Telephone: Extension 64

Completely equipped laundry on the premises for service of guests.

Magazines, Books and Newspapers
NEWS STAND JUST TO RIGHT OF CONNECTICUT AVENUE ENTRANCE LOBBY

Telephone: Extension 46

Maid Service
Telephone: Extension 20

Competent maids available for packing, unpacking and other services. Continuous attendance may be arranged.

Messengers
PORTER'S DESK NEAR FRONT OFFICE

Telephone: Extension 34

An efficient staff of messengers available for errands at all times.

News Bureau
MEZZANINE FLOOR

Telephone: Extensions 6 and 7

Supplying particular information concerning guests to the press.

Notary Public
PUBLIC STENOGRAPHER'S OFFICE OR EXECUTIVE OFFICE ON THE MEZZANINE

Telephone: Extension 59
Telephone: Extension 4

Photographers
MEZZANINE FLOOR

Telephone: Extension 11

Harris & Ewing studio serves as official photographers for The Mayflower.

Railroad Tickets
PORTER'S DESK NEAR FRONT OFFICE

Telephone: Extension 34

Restaurants
THE PRESIDENTIAL DINING ROOM—MAIN FLOOR

Entered from the Main Lobby and Promenade.

Breakfast
Luncheon } a la carte service.
Dinner

The Mayflower Co[...] plays during the lun[...] ner hours.

THE PALM COURT [...] MAIN FL[...]

Entered from the M[...] Promenade.

Tea dances on V[...] Saturday afternoons [...] son from 4:30 to 6:2[...]

THE COFFEE SHOP
MAIN FLOOR

Offering club breakfasts, table d'hote lunches, and table d'hote dinners, in addition to the delightful a la carte menu.

Room Service
Telephone: Extension 32 and 33

A la carte service in guests' rooms from 7 a. m. to 1 a. m.

Social Bureau
MEZZANINE FLOOR

Telephone: Extension 15

Expert aid rendered on the general management of all social functions at The Mayflower.

Stenographer
MEZZANINE FLOOR

Telephone: Extension 59

Available at all times for guests desiring clerical service or that of a notary public.

Telegraph Service
MAIN LOBBY ADJOINING FRONT OFFICE

WESTERN UNION
Telephone: Extension 51

POSTAL TELEGRAPH
Telephone: Extension 52

Telephones
OFF MAIN LOBBY NEAR ELEVATORS

Private booths and courteous attention for local or long distance calls.

Theatre Tickets
FRONT OF MAIN LOBBY

Telephone: Extension 46

Choice tickets to theatres, concerts, operas and all public entertainments may be secured.

Tobacco
MAIN LOBBY AT CONNECTICUT AVENUE ENTRANCE

Telephone: Extension 46

The Humidor has a complete stock of cigars, cigarettes and other smokers' supplies.

Travel Information
Telephone: Extension 101

JUST TO LEFT OF CONNECTICUT AVENUE ENTRANCE LOBBY

Ask Mr. Foster Travel Service. Supplying information and service about air, steamship, railroad and

The Mayflower offered more than usual service to its distinguished array of guests.

The Mayflower flower shop, pictured in this richly detailed photo by renowned Washington photographer Horydczak shortly after opening in 1925, is still in operation today. An early ad in the Mayflower's Log stated that "When Washington hostesses think of entertaining, one of the first steps is to consult with 'The Mayflower Florist.' Whether the occasion is a formal dinner, debutante ball, or quiet home celebration, floral artists from this institution assure those deft touches that bring wondrous admiration." In its early days, under the "direct management of The Mayflower" and its manager Mrs. Frances E. Foltz, the shop promised that the "reputation and responsibility of Washington's Finest Hotel accompanies every delivery."

This 1941 map shows The Mayflower enlarged for emphasis next to an embellished notation near the center which reads, "The Mayflower—Around the corner from 'most everything in Washington."

In 1929, when this photo was taken, The Mayflower appears as if she has occupied the spot for decades rather than just four years. One of the automotive industry's early buses is parked out front, and cars are a blur on busy Connecticut, but streetcar rails still dominate the thoroughfare. Photo courtesy of the author.

This elegant 1928 brochure (cover and interior pages shown at left) captured the ambiance of the hotel itself. The now-anonymous author described "esthetic" Washington and its transcendent hostess, The Mayflower, in words as true today as they were three-quarters of a century ago: "In the foreground of Washington's impressive setting, with its richly historic atmosphere, is focussed vividly the political, diplomatic and fashionable life of the present time. America's civilization flowers nowhere more beautifully than in the nation's capital. . . . The ideal underlying The Mayflower was to interpret faithfully this spirit of Washington. In dignity, in splendor, in hospitality, in service, it has aspired to reflect in the finest manner these high attributes."

A 1930s billboard touts The Mayflower as "Washington's Finest Hotel" and, at $4 for a single room, "worth the difference." Photo courtesy of Frank Fleming.

The Hotel Walker

Mayflower builder Allan E. Walker was a prominent businessman and city booster who had already developed the prosperous Brookland area of the city as well as large areas of northwest Washington during the boom following World War I. Described by his family as a workaholic, he "had faith in the ultimate future of Washington, and it was upon this basis that he predicated all his ideas," stated an article in the *Washington Evening Star*, May 15, 1925. Born on May 25, 1880, he began his career as a teenager working for his father, Redford W. Walker. Despite the financial independence of his family, he was determined to make it on his own and went into business for himself. Before long, he was president of both a real estate and an investment company bearing his name, as well as the

Loughboro Development Company. One of the first Washingtonians to enter the auto fuel field, he was also president of the Washington Fuel and Oil Company and had started a chain of automobile accessory stores. His next project was to be a grand hotel that would bear his name: The Hotel Walker.

Only an underground stream and the forces of nature finally stopped him. Just a few months before it opened, unforeseen construction costs forced him to turn over controlling interest to his creditors. The loss cost him not only his dream but also most of his hard-earned fortune. In a recent interview, his granddaughter, Katherine Braxton Walker Butterfield, stated, "The loss of the hotel ruined him financially and changed the history of the family."

His dream may have also cost him his life. Walker died May 14, 1925, of a heart attack, just ten days before his forty-fifth birthday and less than three months after The Mayflower's precedent-setting opening. He left behind his widow, Maude Katherine Entwisle Walker, and six children. The youngest, Mary Katherine, born in 1924, was only nine months old when her father died.

Katherine Butterfield relates that it is now uncertain how the family supported itself after Walker's death, but anecdotal family history indicates that, from that point on, it was hand to mouth. Walker descendants speculate that most likely Maude Walker relied on her oldest son Albert, who was in his twenties and apparently took over what was left of his father's development and real estate business. Maude Walker died in 1958.

Ironically, even though she grew up only ten blocks from The Mayflower, Walker's granddaughter Katherine was a teenager before she knew her family's connection to it. "I was never taken there as a child to see it," she remembers. "I found out in my teens just by chance because I used to go to the debutante parties there." Butterfield has the sense that it was just too painful for the family to talk about. It was not until 1993 at the death of her father, Allan Walker Jr., that Butterfield learned more. She explains, "When my father died, we inherited these books." The books she is referring to are copies of The Mayflower history written in 1987 by Judith R. Cohen, wife of Richard Cohen, one of the four Washington men who bought and restored the hotel in later years.

According to the last surviving daughter, Mary Katherine Walker, there is one puzzling error in its pages. In one section highlighting "Special Women at the

Allan Elliott Walker was born May 25, 1880, in Washington, D.C. He was the son of Redford Watkinson Walker and Phebe Ann Elliott (Walker). Shown here in his office, circa 1910, Walker was one of Washington's most prominent real estate developers and builders. Educated at Columbian (now George Washington) University, he began his career in the employ of his father. He soon branched out for himself and was president of the Allan E. Walker Investment Co., the Allan E. Walker Real Estate Co., the Bethesda Blue Granite Co., the Washington Fuel and Oil Co., and the Loughboro Development Co. Photo by Clinedinst Studio, courtesy of the Walker family.

Allan E. Walker went bankrupt with the hotel undertaking and, three months after the hotel opened, he collapsed and died of a heart attack just days before his forty-fifth birthday. For days afterward, local newspapers carried accounts of his death and tributes from fellow businessmen. The May 15, 1925, Washington Evening Star stated that Walker was "one of Washington's most prominent business men and a pioneer in the modern development of the National Capital," but that "probably his greatest undertaking was the new Mayflower Hotel, formerly known as the Walker Hotel. At the opening of the Mayflower not long ago Senators, Representatives, local officials and business men paid tributes in their addresses to the courage and foresight of Mr. Walker in erecting one of the most magnificent hotels in the country." Photo by Harris & Ewing, courtesy of the Walker family.

Mayflower," there is a detailed description of one "Evelyn (Evie) Robert, wife of Lawrence Wood Robert, Secretary of the Democratic National Committee and Assistant Secretary of the Treasury from 1933 to 1936." The book states that she was the "daughter of the original, stymied Mayflower builder, Allan E. Walker," and that she "lived at the hotel for more than forty years until her death in 1972." A most colorful character, the book states, "she was once voted 'Miss Mayflower' by the hotel staff for her largesse. A great lover of animals, she not only worked for the city's zoo but also occasionally kept lion cubs in her apartment and walked through the lobby with an alligator on a leash."

Mary Katherine Walker, left, is the only surviving daughter of Mayflower builder Allan E. Walker. Only nine months old when her father died suddenly, she had never set foot in The Mayflower until April 14, 2000—the year of the hotel's seventy-fifth birthday—when she and her niece Katherine "Kay" Braxton Walker Butterfield, right, were hosted by the hotel for lunch. Photo by the author.

Mary Katherine Walker states unequivocally, "I never had a sister named Evie, and if she lived in The Mayflower, I would have known." Mary says that her father "told Mother he had fixed up an apartment that we were going to move into right off the lobby of the hotel." Another daughter, Phebe, alluded to window seats near what was to have been their new home. Most likely the apartment's location was actually on the mezzanine, where the window seats remain. Katherine Butterfield can think of only one explanation for the confusion: "Maybe this Evie was the one who wound up living in the apartment my grandfather promised to my grandmother."

Research underscores that explanation. Evie Robert's maiden name was also Walker. A photo in the November 1927 *Mayflower's Log* shows "Miss Evelyn Walker, debutante daughter of Mr. and Mrs. Harold Walker, for whom they will give a ball at The Mayflower on December 21." This is the same Evelyn who would marry Lawrence Wood Robert in another signature Mayflower social event. In neither the obituary of builder Allan Walker nor in genealogies provided by the family is there listed a Harold or Evelyn Walker. While Evelyn "Evie" Walker Robert was apparently no relation, one could hardly blame her for finding a special kinship with the man with whom she shared a name and a passion for The Mayflower that endured until they died.

The King and Queen of England pass by an early Mayflower.

CHAPTER 2

Residence of Presidents
Belle of the Ball

". . . the loyall subjects of our dread sovereigne Lord King James . . .
of great Britaine, Franc, & Ireland . . . convenant and combine ourselves
together into a civil Body Politick . . . to enact, constitute, and frame, such
just and equal Laws, Ordinances, Acts, Constitutions and Offices . . . as shall
be thought most meet and convenient for the General Good of the Colony. . . ."
—The Mayflower Compact

Polished to perfection and having proved her worthiness to a throng of fifteen hundred guests at her grand opening February 18, 1925, The Mayflower was ready for the ultimate voyage just two weeks later. The true test of The Mayflower's launch, described by one *Mayflower's Log* writer "on the uncertain seas of Hoteldom," was President Calvin Coolidge's Charity Inaugural. States the February 1940 *Log*, "The Charity Ball on March 4, 1925, which supplanted the Inaugural Balls of former years, was the first official function at the hotel. It marked the formal induction into office of Calvin Coolidge at the beginning of his full term in office following the year and a half he was President in filling the unexpired term of President Warren G. Harding. Vice-President Charles G. Dawes and Mrs. Dawes' arrival marked the beginning of the function attended by approximately 5,000 persons from all parts of the country. An impressive entrance was made by the Governors of States with the beating of drums and a fanfare of trumpets as each one was conducted by an aide to the receiving group headed by Mrs. John Allan Dougherty, chairman of the Ball Committee."

Robert Beresford uniquely described the event through his eyes as designer and architect:

From the top of these steps [at the entrance to the Promenade] is an excellent vantage point from which to see and been seen, and this was effectively made use of on the occasion of the Charity Inaugural Ball. . . . During the evening the Vice-President, the governors [nineteen] of the various states and other high officials were admitted through the Connecticut Avenue entrance after the guests had assembled in the palm court and ballroom. As each dignitary arrived he was escorted through the main lobby to the head of this short flight of stairs. Here he

Six thousand guests crowd The Mayflower ballroom at Calvin Coolidge's Charity Inaugural Ball on March 4, 1925, the first official political event at the hotel. Mourning the death of his sixteen-year-old son, John Calvin Jr., from blood poisoning, the president chose not to attend, instead sending Vice-President Charles Dawes and his wife, the former Caro Blymyer, his college sweetheart, in his place. Dawes held his own measure of celebrity. Early that year he had won the Nobel Prize for Peace for his work as chief architect of the Dawes Plan, which reorganized the German war reparations debt to the allied nations, to make it more possible for Germany to pay.

was halted while a fanfare was sounded by trumpeters, after which to the music of his state anthem he marched through the palm court and promenade and into the ballroom where a box was in reserve for him.

The final figures blur between the various written accounts of the evening, but supposedly before the night was over, the four thousand invited guests had swelled to six thousand, many probably as anxious to see at last the hotel elegant and expansive enough for the occasion as they were to attend the inaugural ball itself. Too crowded for dancing, they were content to see and be seen. The ball raised $40,000 for charity despite the fact that the president himself did not attend. He was mourning the death of his sixteen-year-old son from blood poisoning.

There was no time for The Mayflower to bask in its success, however. Three days after the inaugural, the hotel hosted the Women's National Democratic Club on March 7. And Vice President and Mrs. Dawes made another appearance in less than two weeks as guests of honor, with

> ## 1941
>
> President Franklin D. Roosevelt announces during a November Navy League dinner at The Mayflower that "the shooting has started" in reference to the nation's entrance into World War II.

General John Joseph "Black Jack" Pershing, former Army Chief of Staff, and Major General John Archer LeJeune, Commandant of the Marine Corps, at the American Legion Ball at The Mayflower, March 17.

For the next nearly fifty years, presidents, vice presidents and other elected officials spent so much time at The Mayflower, they probably felt like they lived there. Many did move right in. After his election in 1928, Herbert Hoover declared The Mayflower his temporary headquarters in planning his administration before the 1929 presidential inauguration, spending ninety days in residence here. Charles Curtis, Hoover's vice president, lived at The Mayflower for his entire term. Even after leaving office in 1933 following his defeat by Franklin Delano Roosevelt, Hoover maintained an apartment at the hotel until at least the mid-1940s.

For some heads of state, monumental but very personal, rather than international, affairs brought them to The Mayflower. Their Imperial Highnesses, Prince and Princess Takamatsu of Japan, stayed at The Mayflower on their honeymoon in 1930.

Roosevelt's vice president, Harry S. Truman, would leave a lasting impression on famed Mayflower maestro Sidney Seidenman and his son, also later a Mayflower musician. For many years until it became too fragile, the junior Mr. Sidney carried a "V-Mail" letter sent from The Mayflower to Private First Class Sidney Seidenman Jr., of the 104th Infantry Division, by his father March 14, 1945:

Dear Son—I just mailed you a box of cookies and stuff and we hope you get it soon. . . . According to the papers, [your] division is cleaning up in the city, and we are praying you may stay for awhile. In the meantime the war goes well and we are holding our breath—I hope it won't be too long before you and I can get together. . . . I played a dinner party the other night in honor of Vice President and Mrs. Truman. He played piano with us (The Fairy Waltz, Chopsticks, etc.) and it was very cozy. He seems a very swell guy. I don't suppose the German Vice Presidential equivalent would go around playing piano with the likes of me, now, would he? That could happen here and damn few other places. Love, Pop

Three years later, the war over, incumbent President Harry S. Truman faced a tough battle of his own, for re-election in 1948. Polls and political pundits as well as the press predicted that Republican nominee Thomas E. Dewey would win easily. At a Jackson Day Dinner in The Mayflower Grand Ballroom, Truman made his own prediction: "I want to say that during the next four years there will be a Democrat in the White House—and you're lookin' at him." The campaign was so close and the press so confident of the outcome, they made an error considered impossible in today's electronic age until, that is, Election 2000. The headlines on election night declared Dewey the winner. By the next morning, a more accurate tally proved Truman had won, and he was declared president in one of the most dramatic defeats in U.S. elections. He celebrated his victory at the inaugural ball held at the same place where he had made his startling announcement—The Mayflower. This event was par-

1942
Spencer Tracy is one of the distinguished guests at the Navy Day Dinner in November.

ticularly joyous, for he had elected to have no ball when he succeeded to the office on the death of Franklin Delano Roosevelt in 1945. Credited with proclaiming The Mayflower "Washington's second best address," even after he left office in 1953, Truman's fondness for the hotel lingered, and he stayed here regularly whenever he came to Washington.

At least one head of state stumbled a bit during his stay. An architectural anomaly in the Chinese Room transmits sound as loudly as if by microphone. A guest standing under the dome at one end can hear every word uttered in normal tones by a guest directly opposite, as Sir Winston Churchill was to learn when he whispered a bawdy joke to a tablemate. States an early Mayflower ad:

Churchill was seated across from F.D.R. at one of those open oval tables they use for State Dinners. It was directly under the dome in our red and gilt Chinese room. The dinner was proceeding very properly. But after dessert was served, Churchill leaned toward a friend at his right and whispered a "wonderful Winnie" joke in the man's ear. Two distinguished ladies gasped. Conversation stopped. And a flush rushed up President Roosevelt's starched white collar. . . . It was the dome: making the same awesome echo you hear when you say your name ever so softly in the Capitol rotunda.

One would be inclined to forgive Churchill this indiscretion on American soil considering his heritage. While researching *The Great Republic: A History of America*, released in 1999, Winston S. Churchill, grandson of the prime minister, "was fascinated to discover that Winston Churchill, at ten generations removed, had not one, but three, ancestors who sailed on the Mayflower and who were among the mere fifty who survived the rigours of that first winter on the inhospitable shores of New England." His research further revealed that through those ancestors, the Churchills are related to at least four U.S. Presidents—Ulysses S. Grant, Franklin D. Roosevelt and the two George Bushes.

Throughout their prolific political years, members of the

Although President Calvin Coolidge was not present for his own inaugural in 1925, the March 1, 1926, Mayflower's Log showed that he was there regularly for other functions. By 1927 he had announced his withdrawal from the next presidential race.

MRS. JOHN ALLAN DOUGHERTY
1868 COLUMBIA ROAD
WASHINGTON 9, D. C.
TEL. CO. 6867

FEBRUARY 8TH

MY DEAR MR. MACK,

YOUR DELIGHTFUL INVITATION BROUGHT A HOST OF MEMORIES BACK TO ME. THE HOTEL WAS BEING RUSHED TO COMPLETION FOR THE INAUGURAL BALL OF WHICH I WAS CHAIRMAN, AND HAD THE WHOLE DESALLE STREET SIDE OF THE HOTEL FOR OUR OFFICES. SMALL MATTER THAT WE HAD TO WALK ON PLANKS FOR FLOORING. BUT IT WAS FINISHED AND BEAUTIFUL FOR THE NIGHT.

MR. DAWES THE VICE PRESIDENT , WAS RELUCTANT TO COME. HE HATED THE CROWDS HE WOULD HAVE TO MEET. BUT WHEN HE GOT THERE HE WANTED TO MEET ALL THE PRETTY LADIES HE SAW, AND WAS AMONG THE LAST OF THE OFFICIALS TO GO HOME.

I AM COMING WITH GREAT PLEASURE AND THANK YOU FOR THE INVITATION.

VERY SINCERELY YOURS

Peggy Dougherty

Mrs. John Allan ("Peggy") Dougherty, chairman of the Charity Inaugural Ball that was the hotel's first official event, penned this note of acceptance to "My Dear Mr. Mack" for The Mayflower's 25th anniversary celebration in 1950. The February 1940 Mayflower's Log recalls that on opening night, "master builders were rushing to completion this great hotel edifice." Mrs. Dougherty's note underscores the anticipation: "Small matter that we had to walk on planks for flooring. But it was finished and beautiful for the night." Her note also provides an intimate glimpse of Vice President Dawes.

clan Kennedy have made the Mayflower rounds. Senator John F. Kennedy lived at the hotel when Congress was in session. Later JFK's vice president, Lyndon Johnson, as a young congressman, also had an apartment here, as did Richard Nixon. Attorney General Robert F. Kennedy was featured speaker at an event at The Mayflower in 1962 where members of the audience included Supreme Court Chief Justice Earl Warren and Washington Commissioner John B. Duncan. Soon-to-be President Jimmy Carter

stayed at the hotel whenever his campaign brought him to the city.

In what could well have been the first sit-in in the tumultuous sixties, Washington's winter weather turned the Kennedy inauguration into a siege. A blizzard in 1961 paralyzed the city, forcing inaugural guests as well as staff to "rough it" at The Mayflower for several days. The hotel was already booked to capacity, so people slept where they could, made as comfortable as possible with warm blankets and sustenance served by the exhausted staff, many of whom pulled triple shifts to accommodate guests.

Vicente G. Gonzalez, who has been with the hotel for forty-four years, vividly remembers that frozen inauguration. Working part time for various restaurants as well as The Mayflower, he was also working as a messenger for a law firm on 15th and K Street. "Mr. Foley [the principal partner of the firm] was chairman of the inaugural ball for President Kennedy. He gave me a ticket for the inaugural at the capital. I was in the stands in front. The steps were covered with ice. I had on three pairs of socks, long johns and my pajama pants and it was still freezing. But I remember those words of President Kennedy: 'Ask not what your country can do for you; ask what you can do for your country.' The sun came out and I was witness to that beautiful historic event."

During the Nixon inaugural rounds January 17–20, 1969, The Mayflower was at 100 percent occupancy, serving as home base for secretaries-elect David Kennedy and Walter Hickel, Senator Everett Dirksen and Governor Winthrop Rockefeller. The February 1969 issue of *Inn-Side HCA* read, "The [Inaugural] Ball was the climax of the social events of the week, and the crowds were charged with excitement and dazzling in dress. There may have been no dancing at the five other official balls, but at The Mayflower guests had enough room to do a mad mad polka to Meyer Davis' orchestra. Exuberant Senator Everett

Dirksen was in good form, and led the guests in an unscheduled group singing of 'My Country 'Tis of Thee,' followed by a rousing version of the Illinois fight song." Just eight months later, on September 7, the senator would succumb to lung cancer.

Vice President Spiro T. Agnew and his wife Judy made their first stop of the evening at The Mayflower, while President and Mrs. Nixon (Thelma Catherine, better known to the nation as "Pat"), along with their party arrived after midnight, all radiant with the evening's festivities. Slipping in the side door, they were greeted by The Mayflower's Managing Director C. J. Mack and General Manager John F. Craver. As President Nixon stepped into the presidential box, the Air Force Band burst out with "Hail to the Chief" and the jubilant crowd cheered and clapped.

Senior Banquet Captain Vicente Gonzalez, with a knack for being at the right place at the right time, vividly remembers a more somber moment in the Nixon presidency, an event Gonzalez witnessed because of the sound effects in the Chinese Room. "Vice President Agnew had resigned. A group of men came to the Chinese Room with Mr. Ford. There were ten people sitting at the round table. I overheard when they offered the vice presidency to Mr. Ford. As he left the meeting, I shook his hand and said 'Congratulations, you're going to be the next president.' He was shocked. He said, 'It isn't going to happen! I haven't taken the job yet.'" But Vicente's prediction proved accurate. Gerald Ford did indeed become president following Nixon's resignation. "I always wondered if he remembered me saying that to him," muses Gonzalez.

The Chinese Room's décor would soon take on more significance than its role in the Nixon presidency. In 1973, when the United States established mutual liaison offices with the People's Republic of China, following what was called "Ping-Pong Diplomacy" between teams of young table tennis players, The Mayflower was chosen as headquarters for the Chinese delegation, which at that time was without an embassy. For eight months they had their own wing, and the hotel treated them as they do all of their guests: they gave them what they needed. The hotel put a Ping-Pong table out in the open area around the elevators for them. If someone wanted to contact the People's Republic of China in the United States, they reached them through The Mayflower switchboard.

On March 17, 1925, less than two weeks after the Coolidge Inaugural, Vice President and Mrs. Dawes found themselves back at The Mayflower as guests of honor with General John Joseph "Black Jack" Pershing, former Army Chief of Staff, and Major General John Archer LeJeune, Commandant of the Marine Corps, at the American Legion Ball. The honored guests are shown here in their box in the Grand Ballroom.

Politicians and the press dine together in The Mayflower Grand Ballroom at the Annual Banquet of White House News Photographers on May 18, 1925. Guests at the speaker's table included President Coolidge, General John J. Pershing, Postmaster General Harry S. New, Attorney General John G. Sargent, Representative Fred Britten of Illinois, Everett Sanders, Secretary to the President, and Robert Denton, president of the photographers association. A similar group of notables, including not only the president but also the Secretary of the Treasury and the Speaker of the House, would assemble February 19, 1927, for the White House Correspondents Dinner.

Of the first of the two Reagan reigns, the February 1981 *Mayflower's Log* carried this note: "Whether you are Republican or Democrat, campaigned for him or voted against him, we were all affected by the frenzie [*sic*] that accompanied the Inauguration of President Ronald Reagan. Continuing a tradition of being a site for every Presidential inaugural ball since Calvin Coolidge, The Mayflower rose once again to the occasion and accommodated between 3500 and 4000 celebrants on January 20th. As if this evening's activities were not enough, the hotel ran at 100 percent occupancy for the week prior to the inaugural . . . testing the entire staff's endurance and skill. As usual, we came out on top and expect to continue as a part of the presidential inaugural tradition again in 1985." Unfortunately, unlike Truman's presidential prediction in 1948, this one would prove untrue.

During inauguration week in January 1985, Reporter Pamela Porter wrote in an article that was picked up by United Press International and carried in newspapers

Photos by Harris & Ewing

A Group of Washington Society Leaders, who formed a committee for the entertainment of the women delegates to the Interparliamentary Union which met at The Mayflower in October

Top Row: Mrs. John A. Hull, Mrs. Charles G. Dawes, Honorary Chairman;
                 Mrs. John Allan Dougherty, Chairman; Mrs. Harold Walker
Second Row: Mme. Wallenberg, Mme. Mathieu, Mrs. John B. Henderson
Third Row: Mme. Riano, Mrs. David A. Reed, Mrs. Frank B. Noyes, Mme. Samy Pasha
Fourth Row: Mme. Enrique Olaya, Mrs. Henry G. Chilton

across the nation: "Although the Mayflower Hotel expects to be filled up inauguration week, for the first time since Calvin Coolidge celebrated his inauguration there in 1925 the hotel won't be the site of an inaugural ball." The Mayflower mystique could not totally be denied, however. Reporter Porter wrote: "The historic hotel will still play a big role in the festivities, housing and entertaining a large contingent of Republican Eagles—an elite group of the Republican Party's biggest contributors—as well as special guests of the president and Vice President George Bush."

Again in 1993, the pull of The Mayflower tradition

In addition to hotel current events, the Mayflower's Log *covered all the news in and around Washington. The March 1927 edition ran these "Presidential Possibilities." However, just months later, Calvin Coolidge, center, had withdrawn and the man pictured below him would succeed him as president.*

proved too great, demanding satellite balls and events. According to the January 22, 1993, *Washington Post*, the "power hotel" during that year's inaugural was The Mayflower, where slumbered such notables as Vice President Gore and his family, First Mother Virginia Kelley and her husband, Dick; the president's brother Roger Clinton; Hillary Clinton's brothers, Tony and Hugh Rodham; Clinton campaign mastermind James Carville; and Inaugural Committee Chairman Rahm Emanuel. Celebrities Barbra Streisand, Little Richard, Linda Ronstadt, Sheena Easton, Carole King, Bruce Hornsby, Matthew Broderick, Sarah Jessica Parker, Macaulay Culkin, Henry Winkler, Barbara Walters and ABC news executive Roone Arledge also chose The Mayflower as their temporary home. Joan Lunden and Charles Gibson, also from ABC News, The Mayflower's next-door neighbor, broadcast *Good Morning America* live from the hotel during Inauguration Week 1993.

Virginia's Democrats staged their own 1997 inaugural festivities Southern-style in The Mayflower, "a restored survivor from a gilded age, full of crystal chandeliers, antique tapestries and a hotel registry that reads like a

1943

On December 15th, Harry W. Colmery, a World War I veteran and past national commander of the American Legion, holes up in a room on the fifth floor of The Mayflower and uses hotel stationery to draft the Servicemen's Readjustment Act, better known as the GI Bill.

Who's Who in entertainment (Kevin Costner, Julio Iglesias, to name two who were sighted)," read a January 22, 1977, article in the *Richmond Times-Dispatch*. Sidney's Orchestra—represented now by Sidney Seidenman Jr., the second generation of talented musicians—once again "hit the standards with style, blowing trumpet, sax and trombone, holding the beat with a stand-up bass." According to the *Times-Dispatch*, organizers had booked the "much-in-demand Mayflower ballroom a year in advance," and even then "had to open up two more ballrooms to accommodate the crowd."

While a move to consolidate and stage fewer, bigger inaugural events in the 1980s would at last trump even The Mayflower's Grand Ballroom and Promenade, in fact, the move to multiple balls had begun long before any perceived Mayflower eclipse. As a January 19, 1997, article by Sibella C. Giorello in the *Richmond Times-Dispatch* points out, "Dwight Eisenhower went to two balls for his first inauguration, four for the second. Ronald Reagan set the all-time presidential record with nine official inauguration balls for his first election in 1980 and

continued on page 36

Fashionable Folk

Mrs. Calvin Coolidge attends a "Morning Musicale", given by Mrs. Lawrence Townsend at the Mayflower— Washington, D.C.— She is beautifully attired in rich rose-brown velvet.

McNaught Syndicate, Inc., N. Y

1944

General Charles de Gaulle is guest of honor at a July 7th Mayflower dinner by the Acting Secretary of War.

Washington, D.C.

Tea-time at the Mayflower finds Miss Angelica Pueyrredon, daughter of the Argentine Ambassador, wearing a chic coat of deep red cashmere with wide lapels checked in black, a red felt hat, crepe frock and matching shoes.

McNaught Syndicate, Inc., N. Y

A gown of black chiffon and velvet, draped velvet toque and a silver fox scarf accentuate the charming poise of Mrs. Woodrow Wilson. Sketched at a "Morning Musicale" given at the Mayflower ~ Washington, D.C.

Fashion maven Julia Boyd found ample material at The Mayflower for her depictions of "Fashionable Folk," which ran regularly in the Mayflower's Log. The trend-setters pictured throughout 1928 included Mrs. Calvin Coolidge (Grace), Mrs. Woodrow Wilson (Edith), Mrs. Herbert Hoover (Lou Henry, whose husband was then Secretary of Commerce), Miss Angelica Pueyrredon, daughter of the Argentine Ambassador, and a Miss Mary Page Jullien. Many of the sketches included the distinct architectural features of The Mayflower, such as the one of Miss Jullien showing the fountain in the hotel's Palm Court, the balustrade of the Grand Ballroom beside Mrs. Coolidge, and a curtained Promenade entrance behind Miss Pueyrredon.

Washington, D.C.

A long panel of black velvet adds grace and contrast to the distinctive wrap of black and gold brocade, trimmed in grey fur. Mrs. Herbert Hoover, wife of the Secretary of Commerce

The tea-hour in the Palm Court of the Mayflower in Washington D.C. finds Miss Mary Page Jullien smartly attired in a frock of beige georgette ~ Fine tucks, a pleated, tiered skirt and jeweled buckles are becoming details

10 for his second in 1984." But in his second term, William Jefferson Clinton bested even that, attending fourteen official inaugural balls. The fact that, after seventy-five years, The Mayflower is the "much-in-demand" spot for inaugural fetes underscores her undisputed title as Washington's grande dame of hotels.

After almost a century lacking public spaces large or opulent enough to befit the "crowning" of a head of state, beginning with the inauguration of Calvin Coolidge, at last the United States, the leader of the free world, had a setting in its own capital city to rival those of Europe and other nations. Though the now-gargantuan inaugural throngs demand equally gargantuan, multiple halls, from the day it first opened its doors to an awed public three quarters of a century ago, The Mayflower has retained her title as the "belle of the ball."

Its resplendent apartments so close to the seat of government and the scene of nearly every history-making soiree' or summit for seventy-five years, The Mayflower at times boasted its own majority of senators and congressmen who became known as "The Mayflower Bloc." Such leaders as the Duke and Duchess of Windsor and Charles de Gaulle would make their way to "Washington's second best address" at 1127 Connecticut Avenue. King Saud of Saudi Arabia and Queen Elizabeth II of Great Britain have walked through The Mayflower's gleaming brass-and-glass front doors. Israeli Prime Minister Ehud Barak chose the hotel for his stay during Middle East peace talks in December 1999. So many past, soon-to-be and future Commanders in Chief would live at this "residence of presidents," as it is now known, probably only the White House rivals The Mayflower as a stage for world events. Above all, it is still the size and elegance of both its public spaces and private accommodations that have earned for The Mayflower its enduring place in the social, political and diplomatic life of the nation's capital.

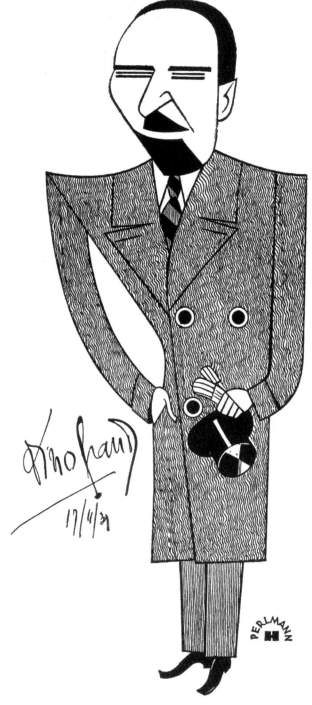

Washington artist Herman Perlman would select only world famous men for the subject of his caricatures. Perlman was praised for his modernistic and original treatment while capturing a striking likeness that usually bore the autograph of his subjects. He made this sketch of Mussolini's Minister of Foreign Affairs, Dino Grandi, during the minister's stay at The Mayflower in 1931. The lighthearted portrait would belie the serious nature of his visit, as recounted by the December 1931 Mayflower's Log: "the Italian Minister of Foreign Affairs and Signora Grandi established headquarters at The Mayflower, from November 16–20, during a period that momentous conversations were being held in the National Capital affecting the entente between the United States and Italy for economic recovery and international peace. The Grandi visit—the latest incident in the new school of 'personal diplomacy' made popular by French Premier Laval's recent trip—aroused tremendous interest in Washington and throughout the world. With the colors of the Italian nation flying over the marquise at the main Connecticut Avenue entrance, The Mayflower assumed recognition as the base of happenings of world wide importance." Both Signor and Signora Grandi relied on the hotel's state-of-the-art switchboard for at least two important trans-oceanic calls—she to phone her two small children, and he to accept a call from Premier Mussolini inquiring as to the progress of Grandi's visit. Management had specially assigned an Italian operator to the hotel switchboard to handle calls emanating from the Grandi suite.

General Manager C. J. Mack greets Prime Minister Winston Churchill as he arrives at The Mayflower for a stay that included a brush with the Chinese Room's ubiquitous acoustics. It was in the Chinese Room that Churchill whispered a bawdy joke to his table mate at a state dinner that was heard by the entire head table, thanks to the dome that projects even hushed tones distinctly to the other side of the room. This and other "History in the Making" events at The Mayflower, such as the day Jean Harlow spent a day answering phones at the switchboard, were captured in a series of Mayflower ads, such as the one pictured here.

Above: Crowds fill the Grand Ballroom at this National Democratic Reception for the Trumans in 1950. Photo by Reni Newsphoto Service.

1949

Secretary of State and Mrs. Dean Acheson and Speaker of the House Sam Rayburn attend the Electoral College Dinner held in April at The Mayflower.

Miss Margaret Truman (right) arrives at The Mayflower with Miss Betty Tyson.

Citizen Harry S. Truman was a regular at The Mayflower even after he left office. It was in the guest book at the main entrance of The Mayflower's Presidential Dining Room that former President Harry Truman signed his name followed by his occupation as 'retired farmer.'

Below: Democratic President Harry S. Truman, right, with his political rival, Republican Thomas E. Dewey, in a more relaxed moment in The Mayflower Grand Ballroom circa 1950. Behind them is Senator Arthur Vandenberg, ranking Republican member of the Senate Foreign Relations Committee and a key supporter of President Truman's Cold War policies. In the shadows behind them is Fred Wiesinger, renowned maitre d'hotel since The Mayflower opening in 1925. Known by all simply as Fred, he had trained in Austria where he had served the House of Hapsburg. Photo by Underwood & Underwood.

Times Herald
SUNDAY, MARCH 15, 1953
These Charming People
SOCIETY
CLUBS
SERVICE

There were plenty of handshakes waiting for guests at the party. In the receiving line above, are (left to right): Gen. Manuel de Moya; Leonidas Rhadames Trujillo, 10-year-old son of the hosts; Dominican Envoy Thomen; the Generalissimo; Felix Bernardino, Dominican consul general in New York; Senora de Trujillo and Senora de Thomen.

"One of the most outstanding fetes of the season was the resplendent reception [right] given by Generalissimo Rafael Trujillo and Senora de Trujillo in the mammoth grand ballroom of the Mayflower hotel," began an article accompanying a full-page photo spread of the event in the March 15, 1953, Washington Times-Herald. Trujillo, by then former president but still dictator of the Dominican Republic until his assassination in 1961, was acting as foreign minister and head of his country's delegation to the United States. The reception, featuring "one of the most lavish buffets ever served," stated the Times-Herald, followed the ceremonial signing of a mutual defense agreement between the United States and the Dominican Republic.

Comedian Red Skelton is one of the surprise entertainers at First Lady Mamie Eisenhower's birthday party in 1954. Mrs. Eisenhower is seated at the head table, far right. One of the other headline entertainers getting ready to strike up his bow was "Mr. Sidney" Seidenman, pictured standing at far right, head of the Mayflower Orchestra for forty-one years.

Left: In this 1957 Mayflower photo, President Eisenhower, left, chats with Lyndon B. Johnson, right, the man who would be president just six years later. Mayflower banquet captain Vicente Gonzalez also got a chance to chat with President Eisenhower, but not at The Mayflower. "I went with friends to see the White House before there were so many restrictions. We parked the car and there was a limo nearby. We approached it and it was just the president and his body guard in a Navy uniform. I said 'Good morning, Mr. President,' and we shook hands. I told him my friends were from New York and we were sightseeing. He offered me his card in case we needed to get in somewhere, but I refused. I was stupid!" Photo by Reni Newsphoto Service.

Richard M. Nixon enjoys the fruit course at a Mayflower banquet in 1952, one year before he became Dwight D. Eisenhower's vice president. Photo by Reni Newsphoto Service.

STATE DINNER

in Honor of
The Vice President of the United States of America
and Mrs. Johnson
given by
His Excellency Fulbert Youlou,
President of the Republic of Congo-Brazzaville

MENU

Apéritifs
Canapés Délices Diane

Le Melon Sucré
Rempli de Fruits Frais et de Baies de Saison

...ms & Humbert

La Tortue Verte au Sherry
Les Piroguis

...ult-
...s
Le Filet de Sole de la Manche, Marquise
Les Courgettes F..... ... ...tits Pois Nouveaux
...chesse

...uile Douce

...ssortis

...Liqueurs
...uillère
...se

Le 9 Juin, 1961

DINNER

In Honor of
Their Majesties the King and Queen of Denmark
given by
The Secretary of State and Mrs. Herter

MENU

Aperitifs
Petites Delices Diane   Half Alligator Pear Farcie
La Ina Sherry   with Seafood Marinee
                                     Assorted Queen Olives
Hearts of Pascal Celery   Pecans

Consomme Printaniere aux Vermicelles

Chateau-Lafite
Rothschild 1954
Roast Bone...
Mint Sauc...
Aspar...
Potatoe...

Mixed ...

Taittinger
Brut 1952
Nougatine Ice ...

Liqueurs
Cigars
Cigarettes

State Dinner

In Honour of
The President of the United States of America
and Mrs. Eisenhower
By
Their Majesties The King and Queen of Thailand

MENU
☆   ☆   ☆

APERITIFS
PETITES DELICES DIANE

Hawaiian Pineapple a la Royale
☆   ☆   ☆
· DRY SACK
WILLIAMS & HUMBERT   Green Turtle au Sherry

Hearts of Pascal Celery   Mixed Queen Olives
☆   ☆   ☆
MEURSAULT-PERRIERES   Lobster Thermidor au Four
1955   Cucumber sur Canape Graham
☆   ☆   ☆
CHATEAU LAFITE   Heart of Filet Mignon Grille Rossini
ROTHSCHILD 1954   Sauce Perigourdine
                    Braised Celery
                    Potatoes Lorette
☆   ☆   ☆
White Asparagus Tips on Lettuce, Sauce Vinaigrette
Bouchees au Fromage
☆   ☆   ☆
MUMM'S   Coupe Praline aux Cerises
CORDON ROUGE 1953   Madeleines
LIQUEURS   Demi-Tasse
CIGARS   Mints
CIGARETTES   THE MAYFLOWER
June 30, 1960

*Crowned heads and
Chateau Lafite Rothschild
were just some of the not-
so-common elements of
these State Dinners at The
Mayflower in the sixties for
His Excellency Fulbert
Youlou, President of the
Republic of Congo-
Brazzaville; Their Majesties
the King and Queen of
Denmark; and Their
Majesties the King and
Queen of Thailand.*

Soon-to-be President John F. Kennedy and Mrs. Kennedy attend a pre-inaugural party hosted by the President's father. In the background is one of the hotel's trademark Tyler paintings of the Mayflower landing. Photo by Bill Rolle & Associates.

1950

The first prime minister of Pakistan, the Begum Liaquat Ali Khan, attends a July Mayflower reception in honor of President and Mrs. Harry Truman. The prime minister would be assassinated one year later, in 1951.

Three of history's notables share a light-hearted moment at The Mayflower in this undated photo: Dwight D. Eisenhower, Henry Cabot Lodge Jr., and Richard Nixon.

The newly sworn-in President of the United States John F. Kennedy greets the throngs of people crowded into The Mayflower Grand Ballroom for his January 20, 1961, inaugural ball. With him are, from left to right, Vice President Lyndon Johnson, First Lady Jacqueline Bouvier Kennedy, Mayflower General Manager C. J. Mack, and "Lady Bird" (Claudia Alta Taylor) Johnson in a white fur stole.

Right: Attorney General Robert Kennedy arrives at The Mayflower where he was to give a speech circa 1962.

Left: Vice President and Mrs. Johnson are joined by Peggy Wheeden (left) of ABC News, The Mayflower's next-door neighbor, in this 1962 photo. Photo by Reni Newsphoto Service.

Massachusetts Senator Edward Moore ("Ted") Kennedy is interviewed by a member of the press in The Mayflower's Promenade in this mid-1970s photo. Also pictured at right are General Manager George DeKornfeld and one of the hotel's renowned uniform services staff. Photo by Youngsphoto Productions.

In the second dance of the evening, President Lyndon Baines Johnson dances with Muriel Humphrey, wife of the vice president, at The Mayflower Hotel Inaugural Ball in 1965.

1965 Inauguration Dinner

Menu

Aperitifs
Alligator Pear, Stuffed with Seafood Marinée
Hearts of Pascal Celery   Assorted Queen Olives
Assorted Nuts

Moulin-Haut-Larroque
Charcoal Broiled Heart of Filet Mignon, sur Canapé
Fresh Mushroom Cap

French Cut String Beans Provencale
Pommes Parisienne

Mixed Green Spring Salad

Bombe Cardinale   Gâteau Diplomate   Demi-Tasse
Mints

Liqueurs

January 18, 1965

The Mayflower

Vice President Hubert Humphrey makes a point during this 1967 event at The Mayflower. Photo by Reni Newsphoto Service.

1951

In August, King Farouk I and Queen Narriman of Egypt attend a wedding dinner and dance in their honor.

Above: Mrs. Gerald (Elizabeth Ann "Betty") Ford, left, is greeted by Mrs. Howard Jenkins at a 1967 occasion at The Mayflower. Behind them is Mrs. Everett Dirksen. Photo by Reni Newsphoto Service.

Left: A special portico bearing the Presidential Seal shelters the stage of the Grand Ballroom at Richard M. Nixon's Inaugural Ball in 1969. Mayflower Senior Banquet Captain Vicente Gonzalez would recall, some years later, the night before Nixon's resignation when he held a farewell for his staff in the same room. Recalls Gonzalez, "Mr. Nixon was pensive, by himself, apart from the crowd. He kept turning around watching."

Vice President Walter Mondale shares the spotlight at a 1977 inaugural event for President Jimmy Carter in the Mayflower Grand Ballroom January 20, 1977. Photo by Youngsphoto Productions.

Right: President and Mrs. Reagan arrive for one of many events he and First Lady Nancy attended at The Mayflower. At far left is Jessie Smail, Director of Convention Services. Vicente Gonzalez, an associate with the food and beverage staff who has been with the hotel for forty-four years, remembers one Reagan event in particular. "The day before Mr. Reagan's inauguration, he hosted a big reception for his staff. I was given a big bowl of Jelly Bellies. The maitre d', Frank Steiner, told me to stay at the door and present them to the president when he walked in and then put them in the center of the buffet table. When I presented them, he shook my hand and thanked me. During the evening the hotel staff lined up to meet him. When he reached me, he laughed and said 'You again?' It was one of those things you never forget. He was a very nice man." Photo courtesy of Jessie Smail.

Inset: Nancy Reagan at his side, President Ronald Reagan addresses the celebrants at his 1981 inaugural ball.

From Dry to Drinks by the Pound

Normally merely a stage for world events, The Mayflower had a hand in at least one historic event—the repeal of Prohibition in 1933. While its afternoon teas, fine dining and stately banquets kept it at the forefront of publicized social events, The Mayflower was losing even the most upstanding citizens and their guests who were flocking to illegal speakeasies where huge quantities of liquor were consumed. For reasons of both business and popular sentiment, it was time for a change.

The hotel served as the meeting place of the Women's Organization for National Prohibition Reform. On March 5, 1931, it also was the site of a pivotal meeting of the Democratic National Committee at which Committee Chairman John J. Raskob insisted that the question of repeal be debated at the meeting, which was broadcast across the nation by radio from The Mayflower. To his

A waitress in The Mayflower's Town & Country Lounge measures drinks sold by the pound. Photo courtesy of Frank Fleming.

credit but also his downfall, party leader and nomination front-runner Alfred E. Smith supported Raskob, stating according to the *Washington Star*, "If the chairman of this committee is to be dragged around because he expressed his opinion, we'd better give up the idea of being Democrats." The paper further reported that "Wets and drys went at each other in hammer-and-tongs fashion," at times drowning out the speaker's words. The proceedings so outraged some committee members that they switched their support to Franklin D. Roosevelt, a defection some historians believe secured him the presidential nomination.

An equal opportunity hostelry, The Mayflower hosted a regional conference of the National Woman's Christian Temperance Union December 4th, 5th and 6th, 1931, "the first of a series of meetings instituted by the organization to promote law observance, to study the problems of law enforcement, and to encourage prohibition sentiment throughout the country," reported the *Log*. Claiming units "in every state and in Alaska, Hawaii, the Philippines, and in Porto [sic] Rico," and part of a half a million members of the World's W.C.T.U., a highlight of the conference was the presenting of the "Youth's Roll Call," a pledge of law observance signed by one million young people.

Just one month later the twenty-fifth biennial national convention of the Anti-Saloon League of America arrived at the Mayflower January 15–19, 1932, where leading authorities on "the liquor problem" debated the prohibition issue in open session and members formulated their plans and strategies for the ensuing two years. Founded in Oberlin, Ohio, in 1893, at the time of the conference the league boasted sixty state and national offices and two thousand members representing the leading church and temperance groups of America. In a not-so-subtle juxtaposition, right beside the announcement in

Alfred E. Smith, in early 1931 the front-runner for the Democratic presidential nomination and an outspoken advocate for repeal of Prohibition, finishes a radio broadcast from The Mayflower with a flourish.

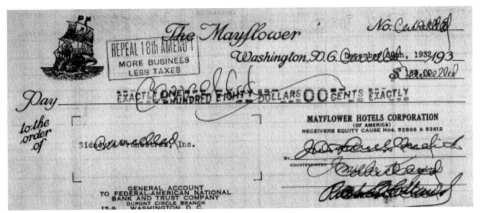

A cancelled check for $180 made out to the Mayflower's "Sidney's Orchestras, Inc." December 30th, 1932, bears a stamp reflecting the hotel's Prohibition sentiments: "REPEAL 18th AMEND'T, MORE BUSINESS, LESS TAXES."

the *Log* of the Anti-Saloon League meeting was a picture of Raskob, chairman of the Democratic National Committee who had spearheaded the heated Prohibition debate just a few months prior.

The repeal platform won and within months after taking office in March 1933, Roosevelt introduced a bill that would legalize alcoholic beverages. Although some states would adopt their own prohibition laws, by the end of 1933 the Twenty-third Amendment had replaced the Eighteenth Amendment and alcoholic consumption was legal for the first time in fourteen years. While Roosevelt is credited with leading the country out of the Depression with sweeping social reforms, with the repeal of Prohibition happy days were here again, and it is debatable which action had the most favorable impact on both the economy and the public mood.

Quickly seizing the advantage, The Mayflower lined up first to pay its $1,000 for a license, obtaining No. 1 dated February 6, 1934 "for a Retailers License, Class C for a Hotel under the District of Columbia Alcoholic Beverage Control Act." License in hand, management quickly opened "The Mayflower Men's Bar" with "Patronage Restricted to MEN." One has to

wonder how those attendees at the Women's Organization for National Prohibition Reform who had so valiantly fought for repeal reacted to this restriction. They would not be granted the privilege of entering the bar for almost another decade. Until then, the world's power women continued to frequent the elaborate afternoon teas for which The Mayflower still remains famous.

Meantime, the July–August 1940 *Mayflower's Log* poked fun at those women who did attempt the hard stuff. It contained this snippet:

If women are going to take it as their prerogative these days to march right into liquor stores and make purchases, we think the ladies should at least learn something about brand names. . . . The other day we heard a languid blonde ordering "Five Roses," and soon thereafter another fragile wisp of femininity said to the clerk, "A quart of 'Kentucky Cream,' please." . . . We had just done gasping at this when the telephone rang and we heard the liquor store proprietor saying, "Country Gentleman? Oh, you mean Virginia Gentleman. Yes ma'am. Right away."

Shortly after Prohibition repeal, The Mayflower opened its very well-stocked liquor locker. Howard Kull is the bartender shown here.

The Roosevelt Reign

The provocative Mayflower muse has inspired architects, artists and leaders, but none more unforgettable than the legendary words composed by Franklin Delano Roosevelt for his 1933 inaugural speech. One would have thought that the forty-eight hours leading up to that moment would have been subdued, even reverent. Not so, according to an undated *Log* article apparently written just a few days after the event. The now-anonymous author details those hours:

Early on the evening of March 2nd, the then President-elect and Mrs. Roosevelt with members of their immediate family arrived at The Mayflower which was to serve as their Washington home directly before occupancy of the White House the same as it had on all previous visits made to the National Capital by the Roosevelt family in recent years.

Mrs. Roosevelt instantly gave Washington an indication of the degree of informality that can be expected for the next four years. Instead of entering the hotel from a limousine in the official procession, she took a short walk with one of her pet dogs. The next morning before the hour that most guests in the hotel were breakfasting, she went for an automobile ride in Rock Creek Park.

In the evening before retiring for the last night that he would spend as a private citizen in a long while, Mr. Roosevelt dictated his Inaugural Address, a document that has been widely hailed as a "Second Gettysburg Address."

There was a spirit of restlessness about the hotel on the morning of March 4th—that is just about everywhere except in Suite 776 where the Roosevelt family prepared for the day's momentous events. The same informality reigned. If some modern Rip Van Winkle had been suddenly cast into the scene after twenty years' unfamiliarity with current happenings, he probably would have surmised that a very devoted family were going on a picnic.

Roosevelt's long-running love affair with The Mayflower began before his equally long term in Washington as president. Photographed in May 1932 as they departed from The Mayflower, the New York Governor and First Lady of the Empire State, Franklin and Eleanor Roosevelt, are pictured en route to the White House where a number of state executives were dinner guests of President and Mrs. Hoover following a governor's conference in Richmond, Virginia. Photograph by Underwood & Underwood.

Taken on March 4, 1933, prior to his departure from The Mayflower to be driven by motorcade to his swearing in ceremonies at the Capitol, this photo captures soon-to-be President Franklin Delano Roosevelt being aided by a member of the Secret Service. To the immediate left of FDR is Ralph L. Pollio, Mayflower General Manager. Information on the back of the photo identifies the gentleman in epaulets and gold braid, worn on the right shoulder, as a presidential aide. Roosevelt is standing at the entrance to Suite 776, where, the night before, he had written his now-famous words, "The only thing we have to fear is fear itself."

Visitors filed in and out. Old friends wanted a last handshake. One of the last to join the family was Mrs. James Roosevelt, whose son in a few hours was to receive an honor which Democracy had accorded on 31 men before him.

Mrs. Franklin Delano Roosevelt surveyed her large family and with a dispatch that would have struck a ceremonial officer dumb began, "John, you stay with grandma," until the problem of automobile seating had been settled.

In a scenario unlikely in today's stepped-up security, Columbia Broadcasting System reporter Ted Church was waiting with microphone in hand just outside Suite 776 as the Roosevelt entourage stepped outside the door and made their way to the De Sales Street exit, to their waiting automobiles and to history.

Prior to this day, the black clouds of the Great Depression had blocked all hope as both bread lines and unemployment lines grew longer and longer. Wrote Mayflower historian Judith Cohen in 1987:

The economic and social climate remained virtually unchanged until the chilly, drizzly, overcast morning of March 4, 1933, when Franklin Delano Roosevelt was sworn in as President. Initially, anxiety hung like clouds over the crowd that gathered around the Capitol to witness the inauguration. Then FDR began to speak in his powerful resonant voice. Words of reassurance rolled out, words he had written the night before at The Mayflower: "The only thing we have to fear is fear itself." The

crowd's ovation thundered across the plaza. As he concluded, the sky cleared and sunlight streamed down on the Capital in a seeming miracle that underscored FDR's promise to restore hope and confidence to the nation.

Roosevelt's long-running love affair with The Mayflower began even before his four-term presidency. As New York Governor, Roosevelt was a frequent visitor to the hotel when he had business in Washington. Duly impressed, Roosevelt chose the hotel to host several major national and international conferences during Hoover's administration.

It was here also that he and his staff of advisers—"The Brain Trust"—had their headquarters prior to his inauguration. After he assumed the presidency, it was at The Mayflower that a succession of conferences set in motion Roosevelt's New Deal that eventually restored the nation to economic health. One such conference, held in November 1934 and attended by two hundred experts on social issues,

President-elect Roosevelt, aided by his son James, departs The Mayflower on his journey to the Capitol for his swearing in. Also pictured are, left to right, Mayflower Manager R. L. Pollio, Eleanor Roosevelt and Mrs. James Roosevelt. Photo by International.

(Left) Some of the 10,000 students assembled and Hollywood's juvenile record breaking stars, Gloria Jean and Mickey Rooney

Pat O'Brien plus white tie

Among those Present

Ten thousand students answered the professor's call to the President's Birthday Ball. "Star" pupils recited to the alumni and undergraduates when Professor Kyser took time out to grade papers. Ranking guest speaker of the evening was the President himself. His voice came to the student body by remote control from the White House after the First lady figured in the official cake cutting exercises in The Grand Ballroom of *The Mayflower*.

Supplementing Professor Kyser's staff of music makers were experts on "cinemaology" from the University of Filmdom and Radio. Their delivery brought forth a happy thought as each paused momentarily on their tour of capital classrooms to impart a message of cheer to the wide-eyed students assembled.

Pictures were made during the Birthday Ball and other important functions at *The Mayflower* during the month of birthdays.

Mrs. Roosevelt cuts the Birthday cake as the official ceremonies preceded the radio address by the President

A gentleman from Kentucky, Senator Alben Barkley, and Olivia De Haviland

The youngest of the "Hardy Family" and Mr. C. C. Pettijohn, host to the stars at The Mayflower

A popular duet—Brenda Joyce and Tyrone Power

was sponsored by the Committee on Economic Security to discuss Social Security, declared by Frances Perkins, Secretary of Labor, to be the cornerstone of the New Deal. When America's entry into World War II became imminent following the sinking of the USS *Kearney*, Roosevelt made the announcement at the 1941 Navy Day Dinner at The Mayflower.

The Roosevelt reign at The Mayflower included celebrations as well as summits. Edgar Bergen and Charlie McCarthy performed at FDR's 61st birthday party, just two years before his death. Over the years, such luminaries of the time as Mickey Rooney, John Garfield, Red Skelton, Eleanor Powell, Ray Bolger and Ralph Bellamy entertained the tens of thousands of guests who, both before and after his death, attended the annual birthday bashes held at The Mayflower in his honor to raise funds for infantile paralysis.

Happy days were obviously here again in this moment of camaraderie at The Mayflower between Vice President John N. Garner and President Roosevelt. The event was a 1934 testimonial dinner for Postmaster General and Democratic Party Chair James A. Farley. Photograph by Underwood & Underwood.

Facing page: The attendance of young actors Gloria Jean and Mickey Rooney and veteran Pat O'Brien in white tie and tails at times upstaged even the President and First Lady at the 1940 Roosevelt birthday party at The Mayflower. Following Eleanor Roosevelt's cutting of the President's birthday cake in The Mayflower Grand Ballroom, ten thousand students heard President Roosevelt's remarks broadcast from the White House by "remote control." From the March 1940 Mayflower's Log.

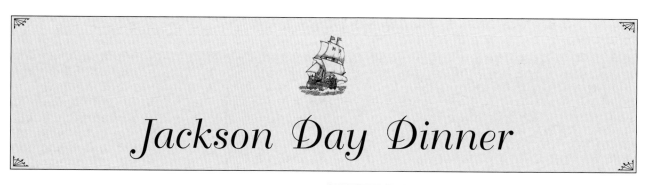

Jackson Day Dinner

For many years, the quadrennial Jackson Day Dinner held at The Mayflower launched each election year's Democratic push for power. The traditional date for the January event coincided with the anniversary of Andrew Jackson's triumph at the Battle of New Orleans and paid homage to Jackson as cofounder, along with Jefferson, of the Democratic Party. It was at the Jackson Day Dinner at The Mayflower that Harry S. Truman announced his intention to run for the presidency in 1948, declaring "I want to say that during the next four years, there will be a Democrat in the White House and you are looking at him!"

The 1939 dinner, pictured here, included addresses from President Roosevelt (seated at far center facing the floral centerpiece), Vice President John Nance Garner, Speaker of the House William B. Bankhead (father of Tallulah), and Democratic Committee Chair James A. Farley. Sidney's Mayflower Orchestra opened the program with "Hail to the Chief," as indicated in the program, inset.

The program for the "Junior Jackson Day Dinner" held at The Mayflower April 19 that same year, proves that emerging leaders wielded their own political clout. Hosted by the Young Democratic Clubs of the District of Columbia, featured speakers at the event included Alben William Barkley, Majority Leader of the United States Senate; Farley; Sam Rayburn, Majority Leader of the House of Representatives; Mrs. Thomas F. McAllister, Director of the Women's Division of the Democratic National Committee; and Pitt Tyson Maner, President of the Young Democratic Clubs of America.

The program from the young Democrats' event reads, in part:

Program

"Hail to the Chief"
Sidney's Mayflower Orchestra

Addresses

Honorable Franklin Delano Roosevelt
President of the United States

Honorable William B. Bankhead
Speaker of the House of Representatives

Honorable John Nance Garner
Vice President of the United States

Honorable James A. Farley
Chairman, Democratic National Committee

Chairman, Jackson Day Committee
Honorable O. Max Gardner
Former Governor of North Carolina

Master of Ceremonies
Honorable L. W. Robert, Jr.
Secretary, Democratic National Committee

Program

Music by
HAPPY WALKER AND HIS ORCHESTRA
Featuring the Hammond Electric Organ

Toastmaster
HONORABLE ALBEN WILLIAM BARKLEY
Majority Leader of the United States Senate

Addresses
HONORABLE JAMES A. FARLEY
Chairman, Democratic National Committee

HONORABLE SAM RAYBURN
Majority Leader of the House of Representatives

MRS. THOMAS F. MCALLISTER
Director, Women's Division, Democratic National Committee

HONORABLE PITT TYSON MANER
President, Young Democratic Clubs of America

DANCING IN THE MAIN BALLROOM FROM 10:00 P. M. TO 1:00 A. M.

In the History of the Democratic Party, Claude G. Bowers said that "where Jefferson had been the philosopher of the party, Jackson became its sword." Together with the immortal Jefferson, Jackson is rightly looked upon as the co-founder of the Democratic Party in the sense that he fashioned the party into a militant political unit that has lived longer than any similar organization in the nation's history.

This program is from the estate of Harold Blanton who was president of the Washington Young Democratics at the time. Photo by Underwood & Underwood Studios; Junior Jackson Day Program courtesy of the author.

The Mayflower Battens the Hatches

On December 8, 1941, the day after the attack on Pearl Harbor, the staff of The Mayflower mobilized, creating its own self-contained civil defense organization to protect its guests during an air raid. More than 300 of the 850 employees, from bellmen and bartenders to secretaries and department heads, were directly involved in the hotel's civil defense. To conform to national defense ordinances, Mayflower management ordered covered the magnificent skylights in the lobby and what is now the Café Promenade (where they would be forgotten and almost lost until extensive renovations in the 1980s). The hotel staged Washington's first blackout drill, installed air raid sirens and first-aid stations on every floor, turned the roof into an observation post and made plans that could convert the barbershop into an emergency hospital on a moment's notice. By the time the war was scarcely four days old, The Mayflower was organized from the roof to the basement to ensure the safety of employees and guests with little or no disruption of operations.

As housing became scarce for the thousands of workers flocking into Washington, General Manager C. J. Mack ordered that the hotel cater to those guests vital to the war effort. The hotel even created the "Interim Club" to serve those businessmen who regularly traveled to Washington on government business and often arrived in the city before their rooms were vacated. These temporary quarters provided dressing rooms, private closets, showers, desks and telephone booths, where the guests could clean up, do paperwork, make phone calls and receive messages at no charge.

The Mayflower became such a nerve center for defense measures, it was considered one of the best "listening posts" for enemy spies

Slick-sleeved young servicemen dance the night away with hostesses at The Mayflower's USO Canteen in 1942. Photo by Reni Newsphoto Service.

and would become center stage for a dramatic event. In June 1942, just six months after America had entered the war, four men got off a German U-boat in rafts and began burying boxes of explosives for blowing up U.S. factories and power plants. A Coast Guardsman on beach patrol accosted the group and was offered a bribe. Instead the seviceman ran to his station and alerted superiors. The four Germans, including their leader George Dasch, fled to

GO ON AND TALK...
I'M ALL EARS!

THE MAYFLOWER ★ WASHINGTON, D.C.

With the increasing tension developing in Europe, the United States began to mobilize its military minds to D.C. in the mid-1930s. Night after night The Mayflower Lounge was packed with top-level officials and high-ranking Allied officers, such as Generals George C. Marshall and George S. Patton Jr., and Admirals Louis Mountbatten and Chester W. Nimitz. So much government business was transacted there, it was regarded as one of the best "listening posts" in the country. Mayflower Manager C. J. Mack became so concerned, he had cards placed on each table that read "Shh! Hitler is listening!" and "Go on and talk . . . I'm all ears!" Hitler WAS listening! In Room 351, FBI operatives captured George Dasch, considered the most dangerous Nazi spy and saboteur apprehended in the United States during World War II.

Her husband's emissary during the war, Eleanor Roosevelt traveled the globe rousing the troops and raising funds. Here she kicks off a "Defense Savings Stamps" campaign with The Mayflower General Manager C. J. Mack. Photo by Joe Tenschert, Tenschert Photo Company, courtesy of Frank Fleming.

New York City, where Dasch confided he opposed the plot to one of his comrades and would reveal it to U.S. officials. Dasch took a train to Washington and called the FBI from room 351 at The Mayflower, asking to see J. Edgar Hoover. Hoover didn't have far to go: he dined daily at the hotel for lunch. According to a March 1960 *Reader's Digest* story by Lawrence Elliot that recounted the drama, for two days, agents grilled the reluctant saboteur in room 351. "A fresh stenographer reported to Room 351 every two hours," Elliot wrote. Dasch showed them thousands in cash to be used for bombings and bribes and provided elaborate details of another four-man sabotage plot in Florida. He also revealed that U-boats were operating at a depth below the range of depth charges. Within two weeks all eight had been arrested. At a military trial convened July 2, all eight were convicted of spying and conspiracy charges. Six were electrocuted. Dasch and fellow German Ernest Burger, who had also cooperated, were imprisoned. Dasch was paroled after the war but was ostracized after returning to Germany, when his wartime activities were revealed.

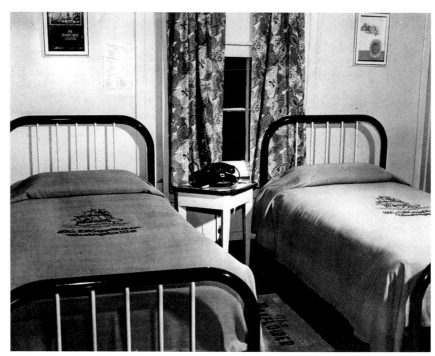

The Mayflower even cast her spell overseas during World War II. Stated a news release by hotel publicist Bab Lincoln, "Out in Kilauea Military Camp, Territory of Hawaii, officers and men on leave are enjoying a pleasant reminder of home in the rest cabins, named for familiar American hotels, and supplied with characteristic furnishings of those hostelries. To the Mayflower goes the distinction of being the only hotel in Washington honored by the privilege of sponsoring one of these havens." Blankets, floor mat and even an ad on the wall for The Mayflower Lounge gave guests a taste of home.

Mayflower architect Robert Beresford wrote in a 1925 brochure: "Connecticut Avenue, the 'Fifth Avenue' of Washington, center of a multitude of exclusive shops, flows past the portals of the hotel . . . ," a statement indisputable given the number of cars lining Connecticut in this circa 1928 photo by Horydczak.

The Company She Keeps
A Parade of Stars

"For we must consider that we shall be a city upon a hill.
The eyes of all people are upon us, . . .
we shall be made a story and a byword through the world."

—*John Winthrop,*
Governor of Massachusetts Bay Colony

By the 1920s, Washington was bursting at the seams. Writes Constance Rosenblum, editor of the City section of *The New York Times* and author of a compelling biography released this year of Peggy Hopkins Joyce, one of the most outrageous icons of the era, ". . . a great many people were terrifically rich, and an enormous amount of money seemed to be floating around. . . . The twenties were a time of sweeping changes that were reshaping virtually every aspect of life. Boundaries between classes were crumbling, bringing a new social fluidity."

In the 1920s, Washington, the nation and the world were desperate for spaces to match the roaring social, political and economic whirlwind of the times. In the first twelve months after its most dramatic debut, Mayflower management and staff raced to keep up with the demand for its accommodations, including fourteen major balls; no less than forty-one regional, national and international conventions; and countless dinner dances, luncheons and meetings. One convention alone—the Interparliamentary Union—brought delegates from forty-two countries.

Although legend now proclaims the Calvin Coolidge Charity Inaugural Ball on March 4, 1925, as the first official function at the hotel, another ball—the Historical Costume Ball—actually preceded it as the first lavish event staged at the brand-new hotel. Held February 21st, in commemoration of the birthday of George Washington, the ball was arranged "under the auspices of the Thomas Jefferson Memorial Foundation," according to the "Souvenir Programme." Mrs. Marietta Minnigerode Andrews, noted Washington artist who taught at the Corcoran School of Art, had founded the Washington chapter of the Jefferson Foundation just two years before. Her home was just one block from the hotel, on Sixteenth Street. In her memoirs, *My Studio Window: Sketches of the Pageant of Washington Life,* published in 1928, she recalled that after World War I, Washington was "no longer the leisurely easy-going town" it had been. The Historical Costume Ball she chaired proved that fact beyond a doubt, featuring hundreds of guests costumed as characters from all pages of history, from immigrants and pioneers to cavaliers, from "The Spirit of '76" to the companions of Columbus. Prominent guests, who took their places at more than fifty historic boxes, included Mrs. Rose Gouverneur Hoes, chairman of the ball committee and great-granddaughter of James Monroe, fifth president of the United States whose term in office had ended exactly a century before.

With a location finally both elegant and spacious enough for real kings and queens and their entire court, Washington grande dames outdid each other booking events for even pretenders to thrones, where even if you were not royalty, you could dress like it at this latest of national treasures—The Mayflower. In the first few months after the hotel opened, a cast of characters numbering in the tens of thousands paraded through the Promenade and into the Grand Ballroom where they danced the minuet at the Costume Ball of the Virginia Society, the American Legion Costume Ball, the Blue and Gray Ball, the Mardi Gras Ball, the Bal de Tête, even the

By November 1926, Mrs. Rose Gouverneur Hoes (seated at left) was kept so busy with social occasions at the hotel, she and a Mrs. Phillips (right), became co-directors of "The Mayflower Social Bureau" and maintained an office in the North Room of the Mayflower. Photo by Harris & Ewing.

Girl Scouts Ball. In its first twelve months, Mayflower management and staff raced to keep up with the demand for its accommodations. Two full pages of the March 1, 1926, *Log* enumerate, in tiny type, "a few of the functions and convention assemblies taking place in *The Mayflower*" during its first full year, including fourteen major balls and at least forty-one conventions.

In 1932, the tone for events shifted from costumed opulence to restrained benevolence as the nation found itself in the midst of the Depression. On January fourteenth, The Barristers, a group of Washington lawyers, sponsored "A Benefit Entertainment for 'The Old Woman Who Lived in a Shoe,'" to provide shoes for the needy, reported the *Mayflower's Log*. In addition to the admission price, participants had to bring a pair of worn shoes as well. Funds collected were used to repair the donated shoes. Gideon A. Lyon, associate editor of the *Washington Star*, used lantern slides to illuminate his talk on the kinds of shoes made and worn in the Far East. "As a special feature the National Broadcasting Company sent its Radiotone Quartet to sing a number dedicated to the 'old woman' impersonated by Mr. Robert M. Tolson, welfare

officer of the American Legion," the *Log* stated.

Equally unique was the testimonial dinner given two days later, on January sixteenth, in the Garden of The Mayflower in honor of Secretary of State Henry L. Stimson by the State Department Correspondents Association. It was the first ever given by the organization, comprised of correspondents for American and foreign news agencies regularly assigned overseas to cover State Department activities. Mr. Sidney and his Mayflower Orchestra as well as talent supplied by the artists' bureau of the National Broadcasting Company entertained guests who included the heads of many foreign missions and attachés. In response to a toast to the Secretary of State, "Neighbor Stimson" (as he was referred to by the organization's president) responded with a brief but eloquent—and now rare—tribute to the American press.

Another history-making conference began in the spring of 1935 when President Franklin D. Roosevelt called the first conclave of conservationists to a meeting at The Mayflower. At what would become annual meetings, the North American Wildlife Conference met "for the purpose of focusing the spotlight of national attention on the problems affecting the conservation of this country's natural

1952

Ethel Merman is special guest at an August Mayflower reception honoring Perle Mesta, U.S. diplomat and socialite, during Mesta's assignment as U.S. Ambassador to Luxembourg.

Facing page: Although the Calvin Coolidge Charity Inaugural Ball now figures most largely in Mayflower history, the Historical Costume Ball on February 21, 1925, was the first of such events staged at the brand-new hotel. Prominent figures attending the ball, chaired by noted Washington artist Marietta Minnigerode Andrews, included Mrs. Rose Gouverneur Hoes (top row, center), great-granddaughter of James Monroe. Photo by Harris & Ewing.

The Historical Costume Ball organizers, members of the Thomas Jefferson Memorial Foundation, used the event to highlight the opening of the intimately elegant Thomas Jefferson Room. Adjacent to the Garden (now the Colonial Room) on the floor below the main lobby, "this quaintly furnished room, dedicated to the memory of America's third President," formed an "intimate and charming setting for private teas, luncheons, receptions and small banquets," according to a 1928 Mayflower brochure. Around its walls hung an exhibition of silhouette portraits of such figures as Jefferson, John Randolph, Mr. & Mrs. James Monroe, Benjamin Franklin and George and Martha Washington, many of them the work of Marietta Minnigerode Andrews, chairman of the foundation's Washington committee and "one of the foremost exponents of the art of silhouette cutting," according to the April 1926 Log. This special room was reserved "for the purposes of the Thomas Jefferson Memorial Fund and the service of the Mayflower Hotel," according to the program describing both the ball and the dedication. The Jefferson Room saw several iterations, from the Pitcairn and Barnstormer Rooms (the party room of the National Aviation Club) to today's Delaware, part of which was cut away to accommodate a hallway to the elevators. Photo by Harris & Ewing.

resources," wrote a *Log* reporter. Sponsored solely at first by the American Wildlife Institute, the conference would return to The Mayflower in March 1940, this time bringing the joint sponsorship of the National Wildlife Federation as well as leading government administrators from Canada and Mexico and the forty-eight states.

It is probably no coincidence that the headquarters for the Washington office of ABC News is located directly across De Sales Street from The Mayflower, for there is probably no other national landmark in Washington where members of the press corps have such a bird's-eye view of the events that shape history. It was here that Charles Lindbergh celebrated his historic flight and where Winston Churchill sat many hours for his formal portrait. Humorist Will Rogers quipped on The Mayflower stage for members of Congress. The Duke and Duchess of Windsor of course chose tea from the room service menu during their stay. Awaiting the completion of construction of their embassy, a delegation of Chinese diplomats occupied a group of rooms for over eight months in 1973. Jean Harlow, intrigued with the hotel's switchboard, spent a

morning as a stand-in operator. Edgar Bergen and Charlie McCarthy performed at FDR's 61st birthday party. A notorious Nazi saboteur surrendered to the federal government in room 351, and Gene Autry, "The Singing Cowboy," once galloped around the main banquet room mounted on Champion. Gloria Swanson, Walt Disney, Jimmy Stewart and Bob Hope all have dined under The Mayflower roof.

Over the years, even The Mayflower staff would be brushed by stardust. Waiter Joe Chapman would play a supporting role in the movie depicting the life of FBI Director J. Edgar Hoover. It was Joe who waited on the notorious G-man every day during the twenty years he ate lunch at The Mayflower. During the filming of the *J. Edgar Hoover Story* in the same booth where Hoover had lunched all those years, Joe starred as himself and provided insights to Broderick Crawford (as Hoover) and supporting actor Dan Dailey (as Clyde Tolson) on Hoover's routine.

The Mayflower stage has hosted some of the world's greatest writers and performers. Nobel laureate Sinclair

Lewis, accompanied by his wife, journalist Dorothy Thompson, "was one of the lions of the evening" at the National League of American Pen Women when it officially opened its winter season in the Palm Court of The Mayflower on November 1, 1926. Over the years, renowned penmen W. Somerset Maugham, Noel Coward, Walter Lippman and Thomas Mann discussed their craft with august Mayflower guests. Composer George Gershwin, guitarist Andres Segovia and conductor Leonard Bernstein joined the hundreds of other musicians whose works thrilled guests crowding The Mayflower's Grand Ballroom.

An eager public clamored for space to celebrate in the now equally celebrated Mayflower even before the March 4, 1925, Charity Inaugural Ball for Calvin Coolidge. While that event is credited with opening the hotel's doors to world history, Washington and the world would not wait, demanding from the very beginning to share this new stage for daily "dress rehearsals" that honed the skills of The Mayflower's expert staff as it marched up to the Inaugural Ball that would eventually, although perhaps unfairly, eclipse preceding events.

But even presidents would ultimately be upstaged at what Harry Truman christened "Washington's second best address," as world leaders—guests at The Mayflower—would

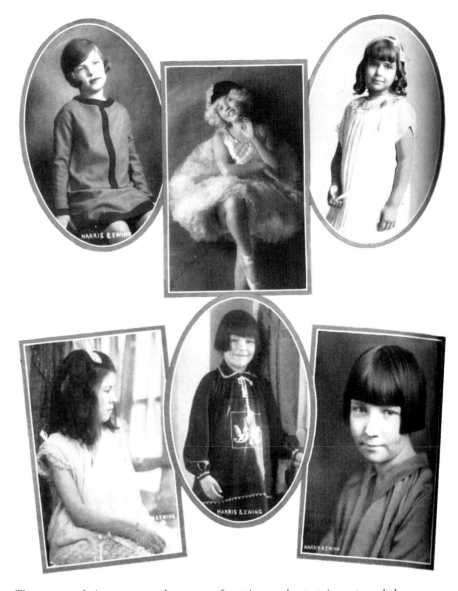

The pomp and circumstance, the nature of meetings and entertainment, and the average ages of its political visitors usually eliminated most little people as Mayflower guests. There were rare exceptions, however, such as these "buds" (a nickname also used for the legions of debutantes launched at The Mayflower). These "Attractive Youngsters at The Mayflower" in 1926 were, top row, left to right: Elizabeth E. Mohler; Helen Virginia Walling of Brooklyn, New York, a striking Shirley Temple look-alike and at the time winner of the National Stage Children's $2,000 Scholarship; Miss Virginia Penfield, daughter of Mrs. Walter Penfield of New York. Bottom row, left to right: Sally Jan Crowder, daughter of Mrs. and Mrs. H. G. Crowder of Illinois; Elizabeth Kudor of Middlesex, Virginia; and Katherine McCeney, niece of Mr. and Mrs. Charles Piez.

struggle to negotiate peace in the Middle East, as Ireland's statesmen met with wizened negotiators to chart uneasy truces, and as China opened its doors to the west with emissaries whose first home was The Mayflower. These words, written in 1925 by Beresford, would become more prophecy than publicity: "In proximity to The Mayflower are grouped the principal points that visitors to the city naturally frequent, including exclusive Clubs, Embassies and Government buildings, wide stretches of parks, theaters and many historically noted spots. Connecticut

Avenue, the 'Fifth Avenue' of Washington, center of a multitude of exclusive shops, flows past the portals of the hotel. . . ." Immediately decreed the political and social azimuth of a portentous century, The Mayflower became a magnetic north of history-making events. It is a magnetism that endures. Connecticut Avenue may have flowed past the portals of the hotel, but not much else did, or has since the day it opened.

The humble potato became the venerated guest at the All Potato Banquet given on March 3, 1926, in the Grand Ballroom of The Mayflower by the Idaho State Society in commemoration of the sixty-third anniversary of the organization of Idaho Territory by President Abraham Lincoln. As recorded in the Log, Nicholas Sabatini, The Mayflower's renowned first chef, was cited as probably the only chef in America who could serve a formal banquet on nothing but Idaho potatoes. The menu included: "Souffle of Potatoes and Anchovies, Soup of Potatoes, Grilled Potato Crust, Potato Surprise, Idaho Baked Potatoes, a la Territory, and Ice Cream in potato shapes." A week before the banquet, enormous quantities of potatoes arrived from the Idaho Falls Chamber of Commerce. An annual event at the time, it was attended by governors, senators and other distinguished Idahoans from all parts of the United States. On display in this photo are special Idaho potatoes, each one wrapped in tissue paper with the name of the individual farmer who raised them printed on the wrappers. Pictured are, left to right: Mrs. Adams Subert, daughter of Idaho Senator Frank R. Gooding; Charles B. Jennings, vice-president of the Idaho State Society; Idaho Representative Addison T. Smith; Ezra Meeker, 97-year-old Idaho pioneer; Miss Toussaint Dubois, daughter of the former Idaho Senator Fred T. Dubois; and Idaho Representative Burton L. French. In a live broadcast, Ezra Meeker spoke over radio WCAP on "Pioneer Days in Idaho." Photo by Harris & Ewing.

Right: Part of the first showing ever in the "Capital City," these two solid gold fountain pins engraved with the ship Mayflower were part of an exhibit in the Palm Court during the convention of the National Association of Stationers, Office Outfitters and Manufacturers in August 1926. Created by the L. E. Waterman Company, they were designed for exhibition at the Sesquicentennial Exposition, in Philadelphia, and after their exhibition at the hotel, they were presented to President and Mrs. Coolidge in special ceremonies at the White House, just four blocks away.

Grande Dames

The Russian Embassy, National Geographic Headquarters and the Washington headquarters for ABC News are some of the Mayflower's esteemed next-door neighbors. The prize for the most patronized—and patronizing—neighbor must go to the Daughters of the American Revolution. Stated an article in the April 15, 1926 *Mayflower's Log:*

"It is in April . . . that Washington begins to regularly prink and preen itself in preparation for the reception of the Daughters of the American Revolution [DAR] which, year in and year out, convenes in the national capital. [S]uch great favorites with the community at large is the great body of delegates annually gathering here, that everything and everybody, from the President down to the smallest shop owner, goes out of the way to cater to their pleasure. Even the Japanese Cherry Trees, sensing with Oriental acumen the arrival of these patriotic ladies, make it a point to throw off their winter wrapping and fly forth, in a bewitching mist, their pink and white banners of welcome."

So, "following the fashion of the day," *The Log* continued, from April 19th to April 24th, 1926, "The Mayflower—Washington's newest and—may we say it?—Washington's handsomest hotel placed itself and all its facilities and resources unreservedly at the service of this distinguished body of American women." With that pledge, The Mayflower threw all its energies into the annual DAR conventions when, each year for decades, four thousand or more delegates descended on the Capital and filled The Mayflower, their convention headquarters, to capacity.

———✠———

DAR President General Mrs. Anthony Wayne Cook (pictured above right), presided over the first Mayflower convention in 1926, while Mrs. Henry M. Robert officiated in 1940 (top left), at the organization's fiftieth anniversary celebration. They were still elbow-to-elbow as shown at right in 1949 when Mr. Sidney and The Mayflower Orchestra played for their dining pleasure at the banquet in the Grand Ballroom. Unfortunately, the DARs felt compelled to move their annual event when the hotel was forced to raise prices. Drawn to a grande dame equal to their own stature, however, they have returned in recent years. Cook photo by Harris & Ewing, Robert photo by Underwood & Underwood, banquet photo by Reni Newsphoto Service.

The first Mrs. Douglas MacArthur, the former Louise Cromwell Brooks, divorced wife of Walter Brooks Jr., was very different in both temperament and taste from her spit-and-polish second husband, a brigadier-general at the time of their marriage in 1922. Daughter of Mrs. E. T. Stotesbury of Philadelphia and the late Oliver Cromwell, she was a vivacious flapper and heiress used to glamorous society cities like New York and Paris. Shortly after their marriage, Chief of Staff of the Army, John J. Pershing, with whom she had had a relationship during World War I, shipped MacArthur to the Philippines. The general was pleased; Louise was not. Although they returned to the States in 1925, their marriage crumbled. She filed for divorce in 1928. MacArthur remained a divorced bachelor for awhile until he fell in love and married Jean Marie Faircloth of Murfreesboro, Tennessee, in 1937. Back to her accustomed high society, the general's first wife appears in her element in this 1926 photo by Harris & Ewing, official Mayflower photographers.

Walt Disney admonishes a traditional "Mickey" enemy as a feline and the famous mouse both perched on one of the original Mayflower mantles that still exist today in most of the suites. Wrote the Log reporter, "The popular young cartoonist who rode into fame with the advent of sound pictures had come to The Mayflower with Mrs. Disney on a vacation trip that had been deferred for more than four years." Photo by Harris & Ewing.

Rules for Long Life

"Much that we suffer today is because of man's sudden rise in wealth and the control of energy more rapidly than he can rearrange his life and adjust stomach and intestines to it. Excesses in the speed of life lead to uneven wear and tear," asserted Dr. Charles H. Mayo in a speech delivered by this famous surgeon at a Mayflower gathering of medical experts sponsored by the American College of Surgeons January 18, 1927. *"Man's struggle today is not for existence, but for luxuries; and his methods of securing them are often criminal,"* he observed. *"Today many suffer from food intoxication (over-eating) and some from drink. The first is slower, but as sure in its results as the latter, but not dangerous to the community."* This Harris & Ewing photo was taken during the surgeon's Mayflower visit. At the convention, Dr. Mayo, who would later co-found the Mayo Clinic, delivered these enduring *"Rules for Longevity:"*

1—*Begin taking care of yourself when young.*

2—*Have health examinations once a year.*

3—*Avoid excesses of life.*

4—*Develop early in life an avocation to maintain interest in the world, preferably along some line that brings one in contact with nature.*

5—*Live in communities protected by efficient public health officers and measures.*

Guests—mostly military men—stand at attention for this photo taken in the Grand Ballroom in July 1927. The occasion was the dinner given in recognition of the first transoceanic flight from Oakland, California, to Wheeler Field on the island of Oahu, Territory of Hawaii, on June 28, in a Foker C-2 Trimotor, flown by Lieutenant Lester J. Maitland, U.S. Army, (fourth from right) and his navigator, Lieutenant Albert F. Hegenberger (third from left). The distance covered was 2,416 miles in 26 hours, 49 minutes. Maitland was awarded only the second Distinguished Flying Cross ever issued, and both flyers were awarded the Mackay Trophy for 1927 in recognition of their extraordinary achievement. Also pictured on the front row, left to right, are: Major General Mason M. Patrick, Army Air Corps Chief; Major General Charles P. Summerall, Army Chief of Staff; Hegenberger; Honorable Trubee F. Davison; Maitland; Curtis D. Wilbur, Secretary of the Navy; General John J. Pershing and Honorable Edward P. Warner. Photo by Harris & Ewing.

Lord Stanley Wykeham Cornwallis, the direct descendant of the Revolutionary War figure, Lady Cornwallis, and a retinue of twenty-seven persons made The Mayflower their headquarters during an extended sightseeing tour of the National Capital and its environs in November 1931. Lord Cornwallis arrived at the hotel on the heels of his participation in the opening ceremonies of the Yorktown Sesquicentennial where he spoke urging Anglican amity. Photo by Harris & Ewing.

Only three years after it "launched forth on the uncertain seas of Hoteldom," as described in a 1940 Log, The Mayflower embraced the latest in mass media technology "years ahead of its time." Pictures in a 1928 ad depict talking pictures being projected before a Mayflower convention group. The Mayflower investment in modern technology came just months after famous Italian inventor Guglielmo Marchese Marconi, in this 1927 photo by Mayflower photographers Harris & Ewing, stayed at the hotel October 18–21, 1927. Winner of the Nobel Prize in Physics in 1909, he was considered the "father of the radio."

The caption under this photo taken in November 1931 at The Mayflower reads: "The world's favorite motion picture stars, Mary Pickford and Doug Fairbanks, were recent visitors at The Mayflower after an extended vacation trip abroad. Mr. and Mrs. Fairbanks came to Washington in the interest of benefit motion picture performances that are being staged throughout the country to aid the unemployed."

An "unprecedented event in the radio world" took place at The Mayflower in December 1931 when Harvey S. Firestone Jr., left, vice president of the Firestone Tire and Rubber Company, signed a contract with Metropolitan Opera star Lawrence Tibbett "by which the famous singer will appear regularly before the microphone," stated the caption to this Underwood & Underwood photo, which appeared in the January 1932 Log. Mr. Tibbett was the first Metropolitan Opera star ever to contract for a sustained series of appearances on the air, sponsored by Firestone. Firestone dealer conventions featured elaborate banquets, pictured here, that challenged the talents of even The Mayflower's legendary chefs.

"Memories of the World War and the international assemblages which followed soon after the signing of the Armistice were revived with the brilliant reception given by the Ambassador of France and Madame Claudel on October 23 [1931] at The Mayflower in honor of Marshal [Henri Phillippe] Pétain and the distinguished visitors who accompanied the one time commander of all the Allied military forces," recorded the Mayflower's Log. Ambassador and Madame Claudel received their guests in the Chinese Room, Marshal Pétain "standing between them dressed in the gorgeous uniform of the French Republic. The chiefs of mission of most [of] the European countries, the staffs of embassies and legations were there, and ranking officers of the Army and Navy turned out in full regalia, their imposing array of medals augmenting the jeweled ones of foreign envoys." Vice President Curtis sent his regrets, having left the city the day before for Atlanta. Photo by Harris & Ewing.

In unusually feminine attire, Amelia Earhart Putnam posed in her Mayflower suite for a formal portrait by official photographers Underwood & Underwood in July 1932. She was in Washington to "receive from the hands of President Hoover the Special Gold Medal of the National Geographic Society in recognition of her solo flight across the Atlantic."

Jean Harlow graced The Mayflower in April 1932. The maze of wires at the hotel switchboard so intrigued the spunky star that she "spent the better part of one morning mastering the system, putting calls through to room service and making wake-up calls," boasted a Mayflower ad not long after her visit.

Foreign flags abound at this July 27, 1937, Mayflower ball, a little over two years before the outbreak of World War II in September 1939 with the German invasion of Poland. Photo by Schutz.

1953

Clifton Webb, Irene Dunne, Clare Booth Luce and Jeanette MacDonald are among the guests at a March dinner given by Conrad Hilton, owner of The Mayflower; Helen Hayes is guest of honor at the Women's National Press Club Luncheon in June.

Shy philanthropist and World War I financier John Pierpont Morgan is surrounded protectively by Mayflower staff as he steps into the hand-operated Mayflower elevator, most likely in the late 1930s. A glimpse of the lobby is reflected in the ornate beveled mirror. A hotel regular, the March 1927 Log records, "Mr. J. Pierpont Morgan, of New York, spent a short time in Washington at The Mayflower on his way south by motor." Photo courtesy of Frank Fleming.

1957

Both King Saud Bin Abdul Aziz of Saudi Arabia and Moroccan King Mohammed V host events at The Mayflower for President Dwight D. Eisenhower and his wife, Mamie.

A personal friend of the Roosevelts, lovely Olivia De Haviland was a regular guest at The Mayflower where she attended such events as the president's birthday celebration in March 1940. Here she relaxes in her Mayflower suite during a photo session.

Van Johnson and Gene Kelly entertain a standing-room-only crowd in the Grand Ballroom during a war bond benefit in 1942. Standing by the piano behind Mr. Kelly, Mr. Sidney Seidenman led the Mayflower Orchestra that evening. Kelly is wearing the uniform of a U.S. Navy lieutenant (junior grade). He and many other Hollywood celebrities joined the service branches in the war. Photo by Reni Newsphoto Service.

Red Skelton, Marlene Dietrich and George Murphy relax between shows at a benefit event at The Mayflower during World War II. Photo by Reni Newsphoto Service.

Actress Anita Louise chats with World War II army officers at The Mayflower, circa 1941. Photo by Underwood & Underwood.

Comedian Bob Hope gets assistance from Mayflower staff during a stay in 1942. Photo by Underwood & Underwood.

Film star Alexis Smith charms her distinguished escort, character actor and film legend Wallace Beery, circa 1940s. Beery made his last—and 252nd—film in 1949, the year he died. The movie, Big Jack, was shot for Metro-Goldwyn-Mayer (MGM). Photo by Reni Newsphoto Service.

Film star Eddie Bracken and Mrs. Jacob Devers almost appear to be performing a duet for the famed World War II General Jacob Loucks Devers, right, in this Mayflower moment in the mid-1940s. Photo by Reni Newsphoto Service.

1958

Theodor Heuss, first president of West Germany, is guest of honor at a Mayflower reception.

Loretta Young and Senator Arthur Coffer were just two of the hundreds of VIP's who attended President Roosevelt's birthday celebration in 1943. Although the president was unable to attend, a cast of celebrities still made an appearance at the annual event to raise funds for infantile paralysis, including Robert Young, Janet Blair, Laraine Day, a teenaged Roddy McDowall and Edgar Bergen. The unidentified woman at left is wearing a barely distinguishable nametag that reads "President's Birthday Celebration." Loretta Young died August 12, 2000 at age 87. Photo by Reni Newsphoto Service.

Actors Paul Heinreid, right, Diana Lynn, and General Alexander Archer Vandegrift, Commandant of the Marine Corps, were guests at this circa 1945 Mayflower black-tie event. Photo by Reni Newsphoto Service.

The heroes sitting at the table in the foreground were decorated by the president with Medals of Honor at this 1945 Nimitz Day Dinner.

Admiral Chester William Nimitz, Chief of Naval Operations, shares the spotlight in 1947 with starlet Angela Lansbury, right, and actress and singer Constance Moore, second from right. The woman to the Admiral's left is unidentified. Photo by Reni Newsphoto Service.

Above: Grace Moore, prima donna soprano of the Metropolitan Opera, smiles coquettishly at Norman T. Kirk, Surgeon General of the U.S. Army. With them is Major André Baruch, better known to most Americans for the sound of his ever-so-famous voice. When radio began in the mid-twenties, the voice was everything and Baruch built a career that eventually ranked him among the legends of studio announcers. He narrated such memorable programming as The Kate Smith Show and Your Hit Parade. Photo by Reni Newsphoto Service.

James Cagney is decked out and slicked back for a black-tie event in this 1947 photo. General manager for thirty years, Corneal John "C.J." Mack would greet every notable guest—and many who would be stars only in family circles—during his record captaincy of The Mayflower. His tradition of hospitality has endured with every succeeding manager. Photo by Reni Newsphoto Service.

Above: Song-and-dance man Al Jolson bounds down the 17th Street steps in 1943 to serve as master of ceremonies for FDR's birthday ball. Photo by Reni Newsphoto Service.

Arthur Godfrey and Mr. Mack share martinis and cigarettes with their flower bedecked dates in this 1947 photo. The event was most likely the "Champagne and Orchids" event, an affair that, each October, opened the "Washington After-Dark Season." The elaborately embossed napkins read, "The Mayflower Lounge." Photo by Reni Newsphoto Service.

Food became secondary to state symbols at this Women's National Democratic Club luncheon March 1, 1949. A miniature Jefferson Memorial dominates Virginia's table (center). A tiny replica of the Mayflower vessel sails toward the Washington monument in the centerpiece of the table from Massachusetts (top left). Kentucky bourbon and thoroughbreds dominated "My Old Kentucky Home's" table 15 (top right), while pineapple and palm trees, a sailboat and seashells beckoned Florida crackers (bottom left). Old Gold cigarettes must have been an event sponsor, for sample-sized packets of their wares were part of each place setting. Photos by Reni Newsphoto Service.

The Democratic women may have relegated food to second place but it was elevated to pure art at the Les Amis d'Escoffiér banquet just eight months later. On November 22, 1949, The Mayflower hosted the world's greatest chefs, where whole game such as deer and pheasant inhabited one of the banquet tables (inset). Auguste Escoffiér (1846–1935), enshrined (top photo) upper left at another banquet November 30, 1952, was known as the "emperor of chefs and the chef of emperors." Escoffiér trained the cooks for the Hamburg-America line and is also credited with training the chefs aboard the Titanic. Besides creating some 10,000 original recipes such as Peach Melba (named after a famous opera singer), Escoffiér directed the kitchens of the Ritz in Paris and London's Savoy, creating public dining rooms in an era when proper etiquette dictated that travelers take their meals in one's hotel room. According to research obtained from Jos Wellman, professional chef and Chef Tutor at a polytechnic institute in New Zealand, Les Amis D'Escoffiér was formed in 1936, one year after the death of George Auguste Escoffiér. Only wine or aperitifs are served at Les Amis D'Escoffiér functions. There usually are no guests of honor, as everyone is treated as an equal. To further enhance their sense of equality, all diners tucked their napkins into their collars to somewhat obscure the differences in dress between those of different income levels. Early photo by Reni Newsphoto Service; later photo by Schutz.

Above: Katherine Braxton Walker, granddaughter of Mayflower builder Allan Walker, enters the ballroom December 21, 1958, for the Washington Debutante Ball on the arm of her father, Allan Walker Jr., who for several years thereafter led the debutantes' parade into the ballroom. Photo by Hessler, courtesy of Katherine Braxton Walker Butterfield.

Left: "Washington's first Debutante Ball, held in the Grand Ballroom of The Mayflower, Tuesday night, November 22, [1927], inaugurated a pleasant custom long a feature of the social programs of other cities but new to the Capital," announced the December 1927 Log. Thereafter, thousands of young ladies would officially enter society at the annual Mayflower Washington Debutante Ball. Among those in this white-clad covey of debs in 1958 was one whose family tree stretched back to The Mayflower's own coming out. Pictured in the third row on the far right, is Katherine Braxton Walker, the granddaughter of Allan E. Walker. Photo by Hessler, courtesy of Katherine Braxton Walker Butterfield.

Each year for decades, The Mayflower hosted the Cherry Blossom princesses during the festival that now draws visitors from around the world. An announcer introduces Miss Virginia as a roulette wheel featuring the United States and its territories waits to the right for the next stage of events in 1952 (inset). In 1963, the princesses paraded the latest fashions through an appropriate avenue of cherry trees. Photos by Reni Newsphoto Service.

1959

King Hussein I of Jordan is guest of honor at a dinner given by the Embassy of Jordan; Mrs. Nikita Khrushchev attends Council of Ministers of the U.S.S.R. dinner.

Rivaled only by the historic Jefferson Hotel just a bit south in Richmond, The Mayflower has been the picture-perfect location for weddings since the day it opened, becoming a family tradition for some. Above: On August 5, 1956, following an elegant ceremony in the Chinese Room, newlyweds Frances ("Frankie") and Fred Pelzman enjoy one last dance in the State Room of The Mayflower before leaving on their honeymoon. Searching for a location for the wedding of their daughter Kerry and her fiancé Patrick Robinson, both in the Foreign Service in Moscow, the Pelzmans again chose The Mayflower for Kerry's wedding May 14, 2000.

Right: After exchanging vows in the Chinese Room as her parents did forty-four years before, Kerry Pelzman and her husband Patrick walk down the aisle for their reception, also in the State Room.
Early photo by Glogau, courtesy of Frances and Fred Pelzman; contemporary photo by Frank Van Riper and Judy Goodman, courtesy of Kerry Pelzman and Patrick Robinson.

Bob Hope, left, and Jerry Colonna, right, pause in almost identical pinstripes at The Mayflower elevators in 1952. The man in the center is unidentified. Photo by Reni Newsphoto Service.

1960

The king and queen of Thailand host a state dinner for President and Mrs. Eisenhower.

Vice President Johnson holds the citation presented to Washington, D.C., Commissioner John B. Duncan by the Big Brothers of the Nation's Capital during a testimonial dinner held January 29, 1962, in The Mayflower Ballroom, where columnist Drew Pearson presided as master of ceremonies. Duncan, "who rose from an obscure messenger in the Interior Department to become the first man of his race to be a Commissioner," was also recognized for his contributions to "the people of all races, especially youth, of his knowledge, talents, and energy." Labor Secretary Arthur Goldberg and Associate Supreme Court Justice Tom Clark were guests at the head table. Photo by Reni Newsphoto Service.

John Edgar Hoover, FBI Director from 1924 to 1972, ate the same lunch—chicken soup, lettuce salad and cottage cheese—at the same table in The Mayflower's Carvery restaurant every day for twenty years. The monotony apparently did not dull his powers of observation however. A 1950s Mayflower's Log carried this account of the day the famous G-man captured Public Enemy No. 3: "Mr. Hoover was enjoying his customary luncheon . . . when between bites he noticed the third most-wanted man in the country just two tables away. With his usual unruffled dispatch, he had the man arrested and taken away. Mr. Hoover resumed his meal." Hoover, at left, is pictured here in 1962 with C. J. Mack. The man in the center is unidentified. Photo by Reni Newsphoto Service.

Desk clerk Stan Anderson checks in Eva Gabor in this circa 1960s photo.

John Wayne lunches in La Chatelaine in 1967. Photo by Reni Newsphoto Service.

Arlene Dahl (left) and psychic Jean Dixon share lunch at The Mayflower, circa 1950. The roses in their water glass was most likely an impromptu presentation from The Mayflower florist. With a townhouse only a block or two away from the hotel, Dixon was a regular at The Mayflower. In her later years, she always made it a point to sit in the area served by Song Kim, her favorite waitress who has been with the hotel for sixteen years. Dixon and Kim often discussed their shared interest in Buddhism. Photo by Reni Newsphoto Service.

Yet another in a long line of fur-clad movie stars to visit The Mayflower, the fastest guest may have been the cheetah Hitari, pictured here getting the hotel's signature first class service. The cheetah was on loan as part of an African Airlines promotion. Photo courtesy of Frank Fleming.

Mike Lambert, right, became the first Mayflower general manager under Westin after it acquired the management contract in 1971. He is pictured here with venerated television journalist Walter Cronkite at the Democratic National Convention Platform Committee Meeting in June 1972. Photo by Timothy K. Judge.

Mayflower General Manager George DeKornfeld greets Nelson Rockefeller, former governor of New York (1959–1973), and former vice-president (1974–1977), circa 1978. Another Rockefeller, John D. Jr.— pictured in inset photo by Underwood & Underwood upon the occasion of his attendance at the dinner given for the President and Mrs. Hoover by Secretary of the Interior and Mrs. Ray Lyman Wilbur on May 10, 1932—was also a frequent Mayflower guest. Later photo by Youngsphoto Productions, courtesy of Jessie Smail.

Jessie Smail (left), Director of Convention Services, and Mayflower General Manager Bernard Awenenti greet Randolph Hearst and his sister-in-law, Mrs. George Hearst, circa 1980s. The occasion was the Hearst Foundation Senate Youth Conference. Courtesy of Jessie Smail.

Right: Hundreds of aspiring actors and actresses bring foot traffic in the Promenade to a standstill as they await auditions of Annie held in The Mayflower Grand Ballroom in 1981. Photo by Reni Newsphoto Service, courtesy of Frank Fleming.

Dave Reynolds, a gifted classical guitarist who now performs regularly at the Kennedy Center's Millennium Theatre, enjoyed a three-year engagement at The Mayflower that he credits with not only boosting his career but also converting him from strictly electric jazz to classical, now his passion. In 1995, when restaurant director Lou Carrier went looking for a guitarist to play regularly in the Café Promenade, the local musician's union referred Reynolds even though his specialty—jazz—did not fit the hotel's gilded colonnades and classical atmosphere. Says Reynolds, "I knew maybe two to three classical songs total." Those got him the booking though, and he secretly vowed to learn as he went. The Mayflower was a crossroads not only for his music but also his career. "I started playing classical five nights a week and put aside the electric guitar. I fell in love with it." So did the hotel's guests, who began asking for recordings. As always, The Mayflower staff obliged, backing the production of a compact disk entitled "Live from The Renaissance Mayflower: An Evening with Dave Reynolds," recorded in 1997. Hotel guests Wynton Marsalis and members of the group Little Feat are among the musicians who received Reynolds' CD when they visited. John Cochran and Cokie Roberts of ABC News, noted Mayflower neighbors, were regular fans. Says Reynolds, "Lou Carrier did the artwork, and the hotel provided the funding. They put me on the map. Without the CD and this hotel, my career would not be where it is."

Lindy Lands at The Mayflower

The Grand Ballroom of The Mayflower would be the scene of celebrations for perhaps the most famous aviator in the world on June 13, 1927, shortly after his nonstop flight from New York to Paris. Breakfast "covers were laid for approximately one thousand people and, in attestation of the unexampled enthusiasm evoked by the occasion, every place was occupied when at the uncanny hour of 7 a.m. Charles A. Lindbergh strode into the banquet hall, accompanied by the Honorable John Hays Hammond, the Assistant Secretaries for aeronautics, from the War, Navy and Commerce Departments," reported the July 1927 *Log*. Unable to secure seats at the breakfast itself, hundreds of other Washingtonians snapped up tickets to the balcony where they could witness the formalities.

At the breakfast sponsored by the National Aeronautic Association, Commander Richard Evelyn Byrd, the first man to fly over the North Pole, read the formal citation accompanying the award to Lindbergh of the National Geographic Society's Hubbard Medal, the highest honor that can be bestowed upon American explorers by the Society. Commander Byrd, invited by Geographic Society President Dr. Gilbert Grosvenor to present the citation, was at the time the most recent recipient of the honor, having received the medal from the hands of President Coolidge almost exactly a year before "for his epochal achievement in first reaching the North Pole by airplane." Besides Byrd and Lindbergh, only five other explorers had by then earned the Hubbard prize: Rear Admiral Robert E. Perry, Roald Amundsen, Captain Robert A. Bartlett, and Grobe Cal Gilbert, reported the *Log*.

The entire breakfast program, including a speech by Colonel Lindbergh, was broadcast from the hotel by the National Broadcasting Company through fifty-one stations to all parts of the United States. At the end of the cere-

This was the scene at the Lindbergh Breakfast, given by the National Aeronautic Association in the Grand Ballroom of The Mayflower June 13. Lindbergh is seated at the speakers' table, twelfth from the left, just below the extreme right of the flag. Photo by Harris & Ewing.

monies, "Colonel Lindbergh amiably consented to pose by the side of a huge replica of 'The Spirit of St. Louis,' done in sugar by the Mayflower chef and proudly displayed by him in the Main Lobby of the hotel." Even before the 7 a.m. breakfast, "the Conquerer of the Atlantic" had posed for his first formal portrait, taken by official Mayflower photographers Harris & Ewing who had captured the "distinction of having secured this initial sitting," stated the *Log* reporter.

One other dignitary registered at The Mayflower during "Lindbergh Week" in Washington—Benjamin Franklin Mahoney, president of the Ryan Monoplane Company, of San Diego, California, whose company manufactured the *Spirit of St. Louis*, and who had also flown with Lindbergh from Paris to D.C. for the event—basked in the glow of courting media and his aircraft's famous flyer. But, while the world public could easily recognize Lindbergh and made he and T. Claude Ryan, whose name is on the *Spirit of St. Louis*, famous, few people had heard of Mahoney, by the late twenties owner of Ryan Airlines. Mahoney bought out his partner, Ryan, in November 1926.

1961

U.S.O. celebrates its 20th Anniversary hosted by Danny Kaye; Sudanese President Ibrahim Abboud hosts state dinner.

Facing page: This was the first formal portrait of Colonel Charles A. Lindbergh after he landed in this country following his famous nonstop flight from New York to Paris May 20–21, 1927. Official Mayflower photographers Harris & Ewing took the singular photo posed in The Mayflower just before a breakfast in the Grand Ballroom in the aviator's honor. The airplane was an elaborate sugar replica made for him by The Mayflower chef.

Mrs. Townsend's Musical Mornings

In December 1926, even the huge proportions of The Mayflower Ballroom were "found inadequate" for the "unmeetable demand" for Mrs. Lawrence Townsend's Musical Mornings, the first of which was mounted December 9, 1925, less than a year after the hotel's own debut. In the span of only one Washington social season, the Musical Mornings became an event no self-respecting socialite could afford to miss. The December 1926 *Log* issued both a promise and a warning: "Filling the boxes and crowding to capacity all available seats in the huge salon . . . will be seen an imposing aggregation of the ultra-smart in the social, official and diplomatic world of America's capital. Not to be on hand at the Townsend Musicales has, indeed, come to be regarded almost as a social *faux pas* and as a bid for permanent inclusion in the ranks of the socially and culturally unknown."

Mrs. Townsend, described by the *Log* as a "nationally known society woman and impresario," was herself an accomplished musician of discriminating taste and a connoisseur of all the arts. Included in the most exclusive social circles in both America and the "diplomatic worlds of European capitals," she was imminently equipped "to carry through with great *éclat* an enterprise few women

would have undertaken," stated the then politically incorrect *Log*. Her annual series of recitals, patterned after New York's then-famous Bagby Concerts, instantly became the rage, especially for the tremendous number of exclusive luncheons Washington's most coveted belles would host immediately following the concerts.

Mrs. Lawrence Townsend, social leader and musician, set Washington's social barometer with her "Musical Mornings." The recitals would become legendary for both the performers and their luminary audiences. Photo by Edmonston.

None other than Grace Coolidge, the First Lady, attended the first of Mrs. Lawrence Townsend's Musical Mornings December 9, 1925, less than one year after the hotel's debut. Photo by Harris & Ewing.

Addressed as "Aunt Natalie" by Richard Crooks (one of her hundreds of artist-guests and whom Dale Carnegie described as the most distinguished tenor America ever produced), Mrs. Townsend became nationally known for her good judgment in selecting artists of established (or soon to be) world renown. For at least the next twenty-five years, Mrs. Townsend would attract such luminaries as Metropolitan Opera star Rise Stevens; dramatic sopranos Rosa Ponselle, Grace Moore and Jean Tennyson; pianist Arthur Rubinstein; harpist Alberto Salvi; piano virtuoso Vladimir Horowitz (who would marry Wanda Toscanini, daughter of conductor Arturo Toscanini); prima donna Mary Garden; and Met star Lucrezia Bori. Celebrated cellist Maurice Marechal, who was among many musicians to debut with Mrs. Townsend, made his first public appearance in Washington December 9, during Mrs. Townsend's 1931 series.

Mrs. Calvin (Grace) Coolidge, described by the *Log* as "always interested in music" and who attended the first recital in December 1925, became the first of First Ladies who dared not miss the musicales. Others who graced these assemblages would include Mrs. Herbert (Lou Henry) Hoover and Eleanor Roosevelt. "Two former chatelaines of the White House, Mrs. William Taft and Mrs. Woodrow Wilson," missed few of the musicals for more than fifteen years.

The artists who appeared in the 1928 season included a young pianist by the name of Vladimir Horowitz, far right in the second row, son-in-law of Arturo Toscanini.

1962

President Kennedy, Lady Bird Johnson and Dr. Billy Graham preside at the International Christian Fellowship Prayer Breakfast in March at The Mayflower; Bob Hope hosts an engagement party for his son; Jawaharlal Nehru, first prime minister of India, attends October United Nations Day Luncheon.

Rosa Ponselle of the Metropolitan Opera Company made numerous appearances at the Musical Mornings. For her February 1, 1928, performance she was accompanied by pianist Vladimir Horowitz. Photo by Harris & Ewing.

Met prima donna Lucrezia Bori performed for the crème of Washington society attending Mrs. Townsend's musicales on January 12, 1927.

Artists in Residence

Its expansive, elegant architecture crowded by both great art and great personalities, The Mayflower muse has inspired artists and writers as well as filmmakers. The hotel itself has been both star and backdrop. Claudette Colbert starred in the 1942 film, *Remember the Day*, shot at The Mayflower, and scenes from the film, *The Private Life of J. Edgar Hoover*, took place at the same booth in the hotel where Hoover also ate the same lunch for twenty years.

With an architectural elegance as grand as the finest museums, some of the most renowned artists in the world were proud to display their works on its walls and in its public spaces. *Mayflower's Log* editor Marion Banister wrote: "The Mayflower which in the fifteen months of its existence has steadily forged ahead as the recognized center of social activities in the national Capital, is now, month by month, gaining in prestige as the most fitting and harmonious setting in which to stage the various art exhibits and other activities of like nature in which Washingtonians are so deeply interested."

In 1925, Nathan C. Wyeth's enormous *Duel on the Beach* drew crowds to its display in the Palm Court. The portrait of Herbert Hoover, then Secretary of Commerce, by Arthur Cahill of California—said to have painted more well-known men in the West than any other artist—drew "much favorable comment" during its Mayflower engagement that same year. And Prince Serge Romanovsky, a member of the Russian Imperial family, "impressed himself favorably upon Washington art lovers with the private and public views given of his pictures" at The Mayflower December 8–15, 1925.

Attracting a cast of painters, performers, writers and musicians over three quarters of a century, while The Mayflower inspired some artists, others made it their

Prince Serge Romanovsky, a member of the Russian Imperial family, gave both private and public views of his pictures exhibited at The Mayflower December 8–14, 1925, just ten months after it opened. Photo by Harris & Ewing.

home. It was in the Mayflower studio of English artist Douglas Chandor where Winston Churchill posed for hours for a portrait the Prime Minister would declare a masterpiece. Chandor would also paint two American heads of state there—Franklin Roosevelt and Herbert Hoover. The *Signing of the Constitution of the United States*, the 1940 painting executed by longtime resident Howard Chandler Christy in his Mayflower studio, would be unveiled in the rotunda of the Capitol in the summer of 1940.

The sea of faces at The Mayflower would allow beloved American painter Norman Rockwell to give visible form to President Franklin Delano Roosevelt's concept of the "Four Freedoms" in 1943. During the war, Rockwell spent hours in The Mayflower's lobby studying types of people and their expressions for the series of four paintings that would appear in the *Saturday Evening Post*. The four paintings—illustrating *Freedom of Speech, Freedom to Worship, Freedom from Fear*, and *Freedom from Want*—were the centerpiece for a major government campaign explaining "why we fight." These four paintings served as the focal point of a traveling exhibition and war bond drive that elicited sales of more that $132 million in war bonds.

However, the work of Dr. Erich Salomon in the 1930s would prove perhaps the most controversial and portentous. The April 1932 *Log* described this scene:

When Secretary of State Stimson appeared behind closed doors of the House Ways and Means Committee to explain the Administration's program for a one year moratorium on international debt payments, members of the committee became curious about the presence of a stranger who appeared to be viewing the proceedings through a device entirely unknown to

Make-up maven Helena Rubinstein (Princess Gourielli-Tchkonia) and her prince (second from right), accompanied by the Polish Ambassador, Count Jezy Potocki (second from left), greet Senator Alexander Wiley of Wisconsin at a March 1940 exhibition of her art collection held in the Promenade to benefit Polish war relief. On opening day, First Lady Eleanor Roosevelt toured the exhibit, which included several Picassos. Photo by Underwood & Underwood.

the lawmakers. The curiosity grew until finally the Chairman halted the proceedings and inquired of Mr. Stimson if the person racing about the back of the room was in any way connected with the affairs of the State Department.

Turning around for the first time to glimpse the intruder, Secretary Stimson replied: "Why, that's Dr. Salomon, and he does not have any business in this room, but he makes wonderful pictures." An attendant escorted Dr. Salomon to the door.

Previously a physician in Germany, Dr. Salomon began taking pictures after being released as a prisoner during the last years of World War I. In Europe he used various disguises to capture the statesmen of Berlin, and his candid photos of a famous murder trial made him such a profitable newspaper sale that he chose to follow the "intimate school of photography ever since," he stated in an interview. He achieved such success that he was invited to the United States by *Fortune* magazine and found most of his desired subjects in America through an extended residence at The Mayflower.

A February 1932 article advised, "Readers of *The Log* will be interested in preserving this copy of the magazine particularly because of the unique examples of an entirely new field of photography." Shunning the long-held tradition of posed photos, for months Dr. Salomon snapped candid photos of famous Mayflower guests that appeared both in the *Log* and countless other newspapers and periodicals. Considered to be the originator of "candid camera," according to a *Log* article, he used a specially designed minute camera without the aid of any special lighting equipment and sought events and persons not

usually photographed. Stated the *Log*, "the fortress of precedents has not fared well with the indefatigable little German." However he was not lacking discretion: he followed the wishes of those photographed and destroyed all prints where the subjects objected. Dr. Salomon may well have been the last polite paparazzi.

1964

Marlon Brando attends the National Congress of American Indians Dance in March; Tunisian President Habib Bourguiba hosts a May 16th reception for President Lyndon Baines Johnson.

John W. Davis, the Democratic Presidential candidate in 1924, apparently was in he midst of engrossing partisan oratory in Grand Ballroom when Dr. Salomon captured this candid glimpse of prominent Democrats of the time. Pictured with Davis at the head table were, left to right: former Ohio Governor James M. Cox, with his hand on his forehead; former Virginia Governor Harry Byrd, with his hand on his mouth; Speaker of the House John N. Garner; former New York Governor Alfred E. Smith; Mrs. Woodrow Wilson, widow of the "War President;" Davis; toastmaster, historian and writer Claude G. Bowers; Jouett Shouse, Democratic executive committee chair; and former Wyoming Governor Nellie Tayloe Ross, vice chair of the DNC and a Mayflower resident. More than 2,000 enthusiastic members of the Democratic party attended this Jackson Day dinner January 8, 1932, at the time a record total for sit-down dinners at the hotel. Diners were served in the Grand Ballroom, Chinese Room, Presidential Dining Room and a portion of the Promenade.

For once Dr. Salomon put himself in the public eye, capturing this 1932 picture of himself reflected in the mirror behind his subjects posed on one of The Mayflower's stairways.

The January 1932 Log caption for this series read: "All of these pictures were taken while the subjects were unaware that this photographer of notables was there." Working unobtrusively and without extra lighting, the photographer, Dr. Erich Salomon, was labeled the original "candid camera" during his time. He found an endless parade of notables for his work at The Mayflower, so he stayed for several months. Pictured, top to bottom, are: Mrs. Jacob Leander Loose and retired Brigadier General William E. Horton; (second picture) Lieutenant Don E. Lowry, U.S. Army, White House aide; Miss Adele T. Jahncke, daughter of the Assistant Secretary of the Navy Ernest Lee Jahncke; Mr. Charles McGuire and Mr. C. Bascom Slemp; (third picture) Mrs. Clarence C. Calhoun, Mr. Clifford Stokes and Mr. Calhoun.

INTERESTING
APARTMENTS
glimpsed at
The Mayflower

No. 1.

The caption for these photos, which originally appeared in the December 1931 Log, reads: "The distinguished portrait painter, Professor Josef Sigall, has transformed his apartment and studio at The Mayflower into a modern Alladin's Grotto. Brilliantly colored carpets, rare tapestries and furniture of superior workmanship have combined to make a dazzling setting for his paintings that are on view." In these opulent surroundings, Sigall painted the portraits of such prominent persons as Secretary of the Interior and Mrs. Ray Lyman Wilbur (also Sigall's neighbors at the hotel), Secretary of War and Mrs. Patrick J. Hurley; the Austrian Minister and Madame Prochnik, and the Minister of Czechoslovakia, Mr. Ferdinand Veverka.

Aldo Lazlo

of London, well-known artist, who spent the greater part of the past season at *The Mayflower* while in Washington making portraits of President Hoover and other government officials.

Autographs as well as captions accompanied these Underwood & Underwood photos of artist Aldo Lazlo, top, and sculptor George Fite Waters taken during extended stays at The Mayflower when they were executing images of several top government officials. Waters not only sculpted a bust of General John J. Pershing, but also a larger-than-life-sized depiction of Abraham Lincoln considered one of the best ever done.

George Fite Waters

of Paris, prominent sculptor, was a recent guest at *The Mayflower* on the occasion of his visit to Washington to make a bust of General John J. Pershing for the Luxembourg Gallery.

The work of one Mayflower guest inspired one of the hotel's own artists in residence. During the stay of Nobel Prize winner Dr. Gerhart Hauptmann in March 1932, Chef Nicholas Marchitelli created one of his masterful candy confections in the noted author's honor. Looking much like a painting, views of both Berlin and Washington were worked on a surface of sugary shield, while a perfect likeness of his famous book, The Sunken Bell, one of Hauptmann's famous novels, was also worked in sugar below the shield. Chef Nicholas' tribute apparently sweetened the normally reclusive writer as well. Branded a blasphemer and threatened with arrest during an 1894 trip to America, the beleaguered author routinely denied interviews and normally took all his meals in the privacy of his hotel suite. Dr. Hauptmann not only ate virtually every meal in The Mayflower's Presidential Dining Room but also granted an interview to the Log's editor as the author was showing the candy-piece to a friend. "Asked if he had been amazed by the changes that had taken place since his first and only other visit to America, Hauptmann replied: 'Impressed, but not surprised. Miracles are expected in

this country,' he explained, 'and no towering edifice of steel or stone should really surprise the foreign visitor regardless of the number of years of separation,'" the Mayflower's Log reported. This 1932 photo of the author and Frau Hauptmann posing with the candy piece was taken by history-making photographer Dr. Erich Salomon, who lived for many months at the hotel.

This Horydczak photo of the Signing of the Constitution of the United States appeared in the July–August 1940 Mayflower's Log. The painting, unveiled in the rotunda of the Capitol in 1940, is the work of artist Howard Chandler Christy who was a longtime resident of The Mayflower.

The Permanent Colony

The Mayflower provided unheard of conveniences in apartment living for residents of its permanent suites, affectionately nicknamed "The Permanent Colony" by Mayflower staff. Working fireplaces, complete kitchens and a private entrance lobby ensured a homelike atmosphere. Servants were housed in a forty-room section in which each room adjoined a private bath—unprecedented luxury for the service class.

One of the most notable guests to grace The Mayflower's 112 semipermanent apartments—called the "Annex" to distinguish it from the 650 transient guest rooms at the hotel—was none other than Charles Curtis, vice-president under Herbert Hoover. For his entire term, from 1928 to 1932, his "suite became the official gathering place of the Hoover Administration," according to Mayflower chronicler Judith Cohen. Because Curtis was a bachelor, his sister Dolly Gann served as his hostess. Occupying an entire floor, Curtis's suite featured "five bedrooms and a library decorated with Oriental rugs and period pieces, including a Louis XVI cabinet with painted panels that was said to have belonged to the great nineteenth-century French actress Sarah Bernhardt," wrote Cohen.

Curtis's sojourn spawned a migration of statesman and, by 1932, twenty-three members of Congress called The Mayflower home. Dubbed "The Bloc,"

this elite list of residents over the next few decades would include Senator Huey P. "The Kingfish" Long Jr. of Louisiana, Speaker of the House and Mrs. William Bankhead (parents of Tallulah), A. B. "Happy" Chandler of Kentucky, John W. Bricker of Ohio, George Malone of Nevada, Charles L. McNary of Oregon, John J. William of Delaware, Arthur Cuppler of Kansas, Carter Glass of Virginia, Walter George of Georgia, Everett M. Dirksen of Illinois, Edward M. Kennedy of Massachusetts, and Edmund S. Muskie of Maine.

During his years in Congress, John F. Kennedy's permanent Washington residence was an apartment at The Mayflower. A responsibility of the senior "shiner" at Boot Black, The Mayflower's noted shoe shine service, was to insure the congressman's apartment had one pair of black and one pair of cordovan shoes polished by 7 a.m. each day.

Nellie Tayloe Ross, pictured here in 1925, was a fixture at The Mayflower for many years during the 1930s and possibly longer, residing in Suite 462. In 1924, she became the first woman governor in the United States. Her husband, William Bradford Ross, had served only two years of his four-year term as governor of Wyoming when he died on October 2, 1924. Ms. Ross had been an avid ally of her husband and had helped him in all of his work. She won the right to complete his term after a special election. After losing her re-election bid in 1926, she became even more active in the Democratic Party, eventually serving as National Democratic Committee Chair. In 1932, she directed the campaign for the women's vote for Franklin Roosevelt, who appointed her the first woman director of the U.S. Mint, a position she held for twenty years, becoming the first woman to have her likeness imprinted on a mint metal. She died in Washington on November 19, 1977, at the age of 101. Photo by Harris & Ewing.

So many statesmen lived at the hotel that at times it could boast its own majority of senators and congressmen who became known as "The Mayflower Bloc."

The Mayflower was the residence of at least one sitting vice president. Charles Curtis, vice-president to Herbert Hoover, lived at the hotel throughout his entire term. A bachelor, Curtis's sister Dolly (Mrs. Edward Everett Gann), pictured at left at the 1932 Bicentennial Ball at The Mayflower, served as his hostess for the myriad social functions expected of a person of his position. To her left is her brother, the vice-president. Also pictured are the Chief Justice of the Supreme Court and Mrs. Charles Evans Hughes; Arthur M. Hyde, Secretary of Agriculture; and Mrs. William N. Doak, wife of the Secretary of Labor. The unusual cropping of the bottom left corner of the photo was to accommodate juxtaposition of other photos in original Log coverage of the event. Dolly Gann was also a staunch Republican, and the Mayflower's Log routinely reported the campaign whistle stops of one of its most prominent residents. In June 1932 alone, her campaign activities included visits to at least five states. Photo by Underwood & Underwood.

Mrs. Ray Lyman Wilbur (pictured here in 1932) and her husband, the Secretary of the Interior, maintained this elegant suite at The Mayflower's "Annex," where they lived and entertained for many seasons. On one typical evening in April 1932, their guests included the Ambassador of Great Britain and Lady Lindsay; the Chilean Ambassador, Senor Don Miguel Cruchaga Tocornal; the Minister of Czechoslovakia and Madame Veverka; the Minister of Denmark and Madame Wadsted; the Secretary of the Treasury and Mrs. Ogden L. Mills; Senator and Mrs. James Couzens; and Senator and Mrs. Arthur Vandenberg. Wilbur, a physician, came by his cabinet post in rather roundabout fashion. He was dean of Stanford University Medical School when the future Secretary of the Interior became involved in the Save-the-Redwoods League. Wilbur was named Stanford University's third president in 1916, a post he held until 1943. The Mayflower made a perfect second home for the bicoastal Wilburs. Photos by Underwood & Underwood.

1965

Astronaut John Glenn is the guest speaker at the Mayflower meeting of the National Space Club, and Charlton Heston takes tea at the hotel before attending the preview of *The Greatest Story Ever Told.*

Justice Benjamin N. Cardozo, former chief judge of the Court of Appeals of New York, succeeded Oliver Wendell Holmes as a member of the United States Supreme Court in 1932. He immediately established his Washington home at The Mayflower. Photo by Underwood & Underwood.

At the age of 60, Ella Loose, widow of biscuit scion Jacob L. Loose, left her quiet life in Kansas City, Missouri, shortly after her husband's death in 1923, and headed to Washington, D.C., to scale the battlements of capital society, she announced at the time. Jacob had co-founded the Loose-Wiles Biscuit Company, purveyor of Sunshine

Biscuits. In Washington, his merry widow became a social butterfly. For almost ten winters beginning in the late 1920s, she held sway in one of the largest suites at The Mayflower (pictured at right), where she weekly entertained national and world leaders and international celebrities. One evening, however, The Mayflower staff committed an unforgivable blunder, according to biographer Wilda Sandy. At one of her dinner parties, they served "a brand of crackers made by a company other than her own!" After her tempest over the biscuit tins, Mrs. Loose packed her heirlooms and moved to the Shoreham Hotel on Calvert Street where she remained for the last seven years of her life before she died on September 26, 1945. Portrait courtesy of Kansas City Public Library, Special Collections.

THE MAYFLOWER'S LOG

INTERESTING APARTMENTS
glimpsed at
The Mayflower

Prominent Washington businessman Milton S. Kronheim lived at The Mayflower for almost forty years and most likely set the record for the longest stay. Kronheim was one of the last to depart, forced to leave when restorations in the 1980s finally ended the days of "The Permanent Colony," as the Mayflower's Log affectionately called them. An ad in the February 1940 Log revealed just how close was the alliance between Mr. Kronheim and his Mayflower home. It read: "One of America's Great Hotels, The Mayflower, features One of America's Great Whiskies—Old Crow, Bottled-in-Bond, 100 proof Kentucky straight whiskey, distributed in Washington by Milton S. Kronheim & Son, Inc."

Aviation Aces and Whirly Girls

On April 28, 1955, thirteen women met on the mezzanine of The Mayflower. They had one thing in common: all were helicopter pilots.

Calling themselves the "Whirly Girls," they borrowed a typewriter and stationery from the hotel and drafted their by-laws on the spot.

The original members included the world's first helicopter pilot—man or woman. Hanna Reitsch (No. 1) was a top test pilot in Germany and first flew a helicopter in 1938. The numbers after an aviator's name indicate a member's chronological place among women helicopter pilots.

Pilot No. 10, Edna Gardner Whyte, became one of only two women to fly the autogyro, the predecessor of the helicopter. The other woman was Amelia Earhart. Whyte had another link with Earhart: she was with Earhart the evening before she left on the flight during which she disappeared.

Whirly Girls charter member Jean Ross Howard (No. 13) received helicopter training from the late Larry Bell, founder and president of Bell Aircraft, later Bell Helicopter. Howard was the member who called the first "hovering" (meeting) of the Whirly Girls and attended their thirtieth anniversary "hovering" held at The Mayflower April 28, 1985. She was also the Whirly Girls' first president.

Valerie Andre (No. 6) became a general in the French Army. A brain surgeon, she was a one-person M.A.S.H. unit in 1950 who flew wounded soldiers out of the front lines in Vietnam, then operated on her "passengers" after landing away from the battlefront.

Charter Whirly Girl Jean Ross Howard addresses the group at their thirtieth anniversary "hovering" at The Mayflower. Howard, a native Washingtonian, as a child perched on The Mayflower's balcony when it hosted a 6 a.m. breakfast for Charles Lindbergh in 1927 after his record flight. It was at the hotel that Lindbergh sat for his "first posed photograph . . . upon his return to America." Photo by Fay Gillis Wells.

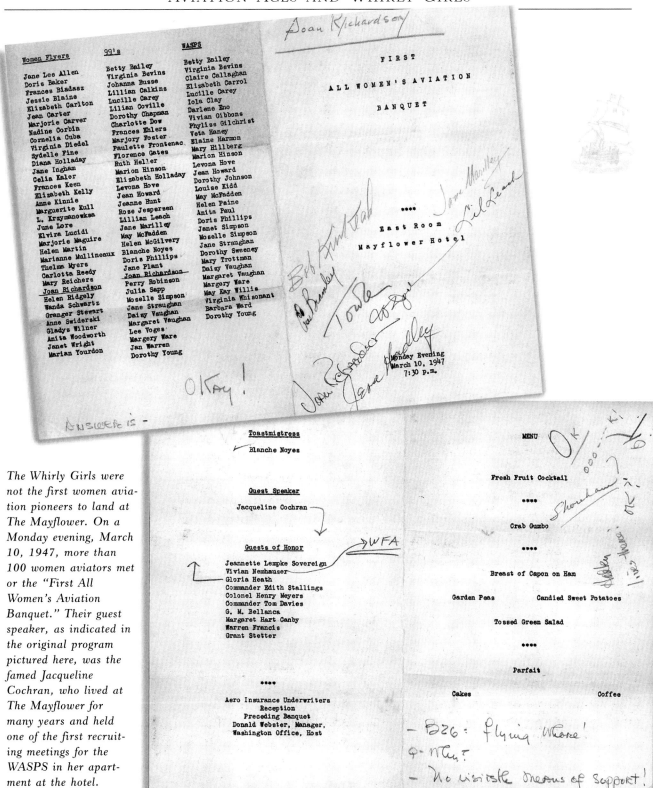

The Whirly Girls were not the first women aviation pioneers to land at The Mayflower. On a Monday evening, March 10, 1947, more than 100 women aviators met or the "First All Women's Aviation Banquet." Their guest speaker, as indicated in the original program pictured here, was the famed Jacqueline Cochran, who lived at The Mayflower for many years and held one of the first recruiting meetings for the WASPS in her apartment at the hotel. During World War II, she became director of the Women's Air Force Service Pilots, teaching 1,200 women to fly transports. She was the first woman to pilot a bomber across the North Atlantic as well as the first woman to break the sound barrier. This program from the collection of Joan Richardson Towel, former WASP and member of the 99s, another famed women's aviation association, bears some interesting scribbles. On the front cover are the signatures of various guests, including one Jesse Hadley. On the inside bottom is an off-color explanation of the nickname of the B26 airplane. And in the upper right are back-and-forth "OK's" for an apparent rendezvous at the rival Shoreham Hotel, with the revelation, "Hadley lives there!" On the back page was yet another "Okay!" as well as the names of all women flyers, 99s, and WASPS in attendance.

Although just youngsters compared to the trio of veteran doormen pictured on page 116, these three are already making their mark as the next generation of celebrated Mayflower bell staff. Joseph Brackeen, left, bell captain, has been with the hotel since 1983. Brackeen is a United Methodist minister with a theological degree. A doorman for over sixteen years, Frank Agbro, center, has been senior doorman for seven years. Agbro is a gifted musician who sings, writes and produces his own music. Besides occasional bookings at local clubs, Agbro's band provided entertainment at one of the many inaugural fetes in 1997. At right, tiny Maria Tung-Maye, from Equatorial Guinea, raises her fist, not in defiance, but victory as the first woman in almost 75 years at The Mayflower to become a member of the bell stand. Maria started out in housekeeping and credits Brackeen with encouraging her to apply for her new position. Photo by the author.

CHAPTER 4

The Heart of the House
A Labor of Love

"(T)o their great commendations be it spoken, spared no pains, night nor day, but with abundance of toil . . . , fetched them wood, made them fires, dressed them meat, made their beds, washed their loathesome clothes . . . ; in a word, did all the homely and necessary offices for them . . . ; and all this willingly and cheerfully, without any grudging in the least, showing herein their true love unto their friends and brethren."

—Of Plimouth Plantation, *the journal of*
William Bradford, governor of Plymouth Colony

Members of the order of the Convent of the Visitation who first occupied the land where The Mayflower now stands remained with the monastery for life, according to Sister Mada-Anne Gell, archivist of the Order of the Visitation in Washington's Georgetown. "You live and die at that same monastery," she explained.

In hotel jargon, that part of both the hotel and its staff normally unseen by guests is called "the back of the house." But Mayflower management, recognizing that both its visible and invisible armies are the backbone of its reputation of service, prefer a modified phrase—"the heart of the house." Sara Moore, director of human resources, was a reluctant interview because, as she pointed out, she has only been with the hotel since 1998. Although, as with every Mayflower interview, her conversation was peppered with pride for the hotel, she emphasized, "People like me are just custodians, passing through. I can't tell this story." She underscores that it is people like Jimme Curtis and Vicente Gonzalez in banquets, both associates for more than forty years, who are the hotel's heart, maintaining a steadfast beat of passionate service throughout its lifetime.

The Mayflower's "heart of the house"—the more than 550 staff members who greet, feed and serve guests and who keep the hotel operating—have displayed a monastic devotion akin to their antecedents, the nuns. States human resource specialist Roxanne Chaclan, "The average length of service is twelve years, and our turnover rate is only 17 percent." Although rare in the hotel industry, where turnover is usually as much as 40 to 50 percent, many of these colorful characters have stayed with The Mayflower for thirty, forty, even nearly fifty years, achieving almost as much celebrity as the guests they serve.

One such veteran was Al Dobbins, a bellman at The Mayflower for over forty-six years. Joseph Brackeen, The Mayflower's current bell captain, swears that Al never missed a day's work. Brackeen asserts in drumbeat cadence: "He arrived at 5:30 every morning. During an ice storm he was here at 5:30. During the snow storm in 1995, with everything closed, Al was here at 5:30." "Somewhat of a curmudgeon," Brackeen remembers, "he used to make me mad but I was sure glad he was here. He was the person who taught me this is a job to be proud of, that you do not tolerate even the suggestion this is not honorable or meaningful."

On February 20, 1999, Dobbins collapsed inside the entrance on De Sales Street. He died that same day, most likely from a heart attack. Brackeen remembers that Dobbins, while not married, often talked about retiring to spend time with his siblings and their children. But, states Brackeen, "He died where he wanted to be, with his friends." Hundreds of The Mayflower's staff from all shifts filled the hotel's State Room for his memorial service. William Randolph Hearst III sent a note of condolence. Senior doorman Frank Agbro wrote in his eulogy:

Al was a true professional who worked very hard, loved his job and took pride in what he did. Al loved people and loved to serve people. He was a gentleman. His view of the world did not end with the diverse nationalities that The Mayflower attracts in its guests and its employees. He leaves behind a lasting legacy of unity, service, honor, pride, integrity and respect for his fellow man. These are ideals worth working for and we thank you, Al, for sharing your life with us.

Al's pal Eddie Derendorf played it safe, retiring prior to his beloved co-worker's and friend's death. "After 47 years of checking in people and potentates," wrote Sarah Booth Conroy in an article in the *Washington Post*, Derendorf retired at age 68. "I decided the time had come to rest my legs. This work is hard on them," he stated then. According to the article, he was the "second generation in his family to work at the Mayflower. His father, Emil Derendorf, lost his restaurant during the Depression and came to work at the hotel as a waiter." Eddie joined his dad at the hotel, first as freight elevator operator and then moving up to elevator starter. But since neither position provided tips, after two years he applied for the job of bellhop, a position he held for the rest of his career.

Derendorf's favorite president was Harry Truman, who stayed in a Mayflower suite for a few months after he left office. According to Derendorf, the former president liked to walk around the block every day for exercise. In an interview at the time of Eddie's retirement, he stated that Truman, "didn't have a Secret Service man assigned to him, so he asked me to go with him. He'd never talk about politics, just pass the time of day, the weather and so on." The day Truman left The Mayflower

1966

Leafold Sedar Senghor, president of Senegal, is guest of honor at the Women's National Press Club Luncheon in October; actor Michael Caine hosts press conference.

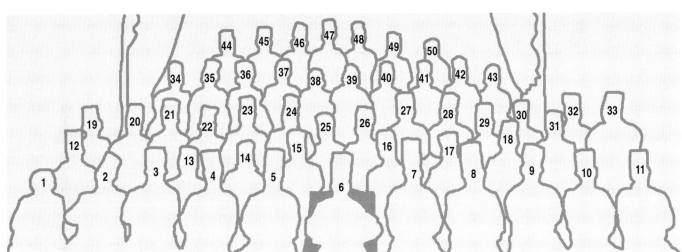

Half of Washington's elite must have gone hungry while the proud "Brigade du Mayflower Hotel" paused long enough for this 1930 group photo (facing page) taken in the Grand Ballroom. Pictured in the center is Jacques E. Haeringer, Chef de Cuisine. The picture hangs in the spartan office of current Mayflower Executive Chef Norman Wade, the same office used by Chef Wade's predecessors. In 1990, more than half a century later, once again the Mayflower's gastronomic masters gathered in the same pose as their predecessors (this page, top). To the left of center is Agostino Buggio, now executive sous chef. All but two in the contemporary photo are identified, although in some cases only by first or last name: 1-Octavia, 2-Marvin Bushrod, 3-Patrick, 4-Albert Stadeli, 5-Agostino Buggio, 6-Michep Trincard, 7-Arnold, 8-Heiko Meitzel, 9-Didier Tsirony, 10-Mao Song, 11-Paul Murtagh, 12-Jose Moreno, 13-unidentified, 14-Abeba Haile, 15- Aloso, 16-Ed, 17-Bob, 18-Emannuel, 19-Maezel, 20-Barry, 21-Wilber, 22-Paul, 23-Leon, 24-Paul Eric, 25-Pedro Rivera, 26- Betty, 27-David, 28-Fred Harriel, 29-Edna Frazier, 30-unidentified, 31-Harry, 32-Hamad, 33-Redmond Barnes, 34-Lois Roberson, 35-Corrine Gomez, 36-Aster Haile, 37-Roza Jimenez, 38-Liz, 39-Flage, 40-Luisa Bernuy, 41-Lynn, 42-Michelle, 43-Ana Diaz, 44-Nefia Escobar, 45-Jay Sniden, 46-Ramon Medina, 47-Gerard, 48-Neal, 49-Asfer, 50-Josephine.

to return to his home in Missouri, he asked Eddie to ride with him in the limousine to the railroad station. With presidential flags flying and people waving, Eddie accompanied the unassuming former leader through the streets of the nation's capital to the station where Truman stepped out, then sent Derendorf back to the hotel in the White House car.

Sometimes staff members are the only ones who recognize celebrities. Recalls Brackeen, "T-Bone [T. Boone] Pickens comes in one night about 10 o'clock. He's making a speech to Merrill Lynch stockholders the next morning. His aide has his boot carrier with the initials 'T.B.P.' on it." Born in 1928, Thomas Boone Pickens Jr., multi-millionaire U.S. oil businessman and corporate raider, founded Mesa Petroleum Company in 1964. On the ride up the elevator to assist with the baggage, Brackeen, a follower of world news and a Pickens admirer, complimented Pickens on his shrewd actions regarding a General Motors failed bid. Startled, Pickens stated to his aide, "Here I walk in to the middle of The Mayflower and the only person who recognized me is the bell captain," whereupon he handed the aide a $100 tip to be given to Brackeen.

Devotion to service has never stopped at The Mayflower's front door. A mid-1970s *Mayflower's Log* article saluted housekeeper Hattie Johnson for twenty-three years of service. The list of guests in the sixteen special rooms that were her sole responsibility on The Mayflower's fifth floor are a veritable who's who of the

1967

Actor Hugh O'Brien is a guest at the May Movie Critics Luncheon.

The caption to this photo reads, "The Captain's Annual Dinner to the crew of the good ship Mayflower to celebrate the Fourth Anniversary of its successful launching, February 18, 1929." At the center of the horseshoe, to the left of the statue, is Daniel J. O'Brien, general manager. The gentleman seated at the upper end of the chairs along the horseshoe's left inner ring is Corneal John "C.J." Mack, who would ultimately become the hotel's longest-tenured general manager. Just to the right of the first flowered centerpiece on the left and across from Mr. Mack, is Nicholas Marchitelli, The Mayflower's second executive chef. Photo by Schutz.

time: "the Shah of Iran, Frank Sinatra, Billy Graham, Rockefeller family members, various U.S. Presidents, Vice Presidents and Congressmen. Add to this a sprinkling of foreign diplomats and other dignitaries." Many of those VIPs gave "generous tips and such small gifts as a personally autographed memento from Frank Sinatra and gift-wrapped testament and Christmas record from Billy Graham." The article pointed out that it was not "just the 'personality' guest" that intrigued her. "She likes all kinds of people, and in particular, the newcomer in town." But it was pride in her work that brought her the most satisfaction. "I like my rooms looking nice when guests check in, and always kept neat and tidy during their stay," she said.

About the same time Hattie Johnson was celebrating more than twenty years of service at The Mayflower, another housekeeper was just coming aboard. Emiliana Mercedez, of Santo Domingo, came to The Mayflower in 1974, her first job ever in either country. In addition to the fifteen rooms she services each day, in more than twenty-five years, she has ironed shirts for a befuddled businessmen from Amtrak, babysat and even, on more than one occasion, retrieved guns left behind by embarrassed security officials who accompanied various world figures. Recalls Emiliana in her lilting accent, "One day I change the sheets on the bed and I reach under the pillow and there was this big gun! It fell on the floor and I was afraid it would go off. I am so afraid! I jump on the bed and call security on the phone by the bedside!"

Her face lit up most when she remembered one special little guest in 1991. A businessman from Africa then living in Ohio was apparently forced to bring his five-year-old son with him on a trip to Washington. "One day," Emiliana chuckles, "he left the baby in the room and the baby went downstairs in the lobby in pajamas." Hotel staff brought him back upstairs and connected him with his father. More than once, Emiliana found him alone when she unlocked the room door to clean. For the rest of their stay, Emiliana watched over the little boy on her shift, bringing him crayons and books and toys. By the end of the week, and to the father's relief, the boy had become her "assistant," following her around as she serviced her assigned rooms. When he left, the father tipped her $80.

As food storekeeper, longtime Mayflower employee Willie Gordon has been one of the backbones of The Mayflower, having worked the "back of the house" for more than forty years, starting in 1958. Early each morning, he saw to it that the many food service areas had the supplies needed to feed—and feed well—the hundreds of Mayflower diners. Ironically, amidst all that food, he sometimes stayed so busy he forgot to eat. But Willie never wanted to go anywhere else because, as he stated in a recent interview shortly before he retired in 2000, "I loved working with the people I worked with. I love the job I do." As testament to the job and the people, over nearly half a century, Willie meticulously collected hundreds of photos, clippings and memorabilia, and lovingly compiled them in several albums as treasured to him as any family heirloom.

Working at The Mayflower even became a family tradition for some. Three ladies, all part of the hotel's venerable kitchen staff, had worked a total of "over 59 years of dedicated service to The Mayflower," according to an article in the *Log*. Adele James started out washing glasses in 1943. By 1981, her daughter and granddaughter, Edna

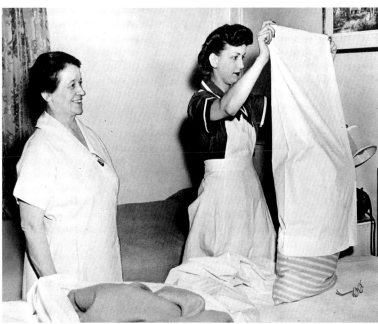

Top: A head housekeeper gives careful instruction to her staff on the importance of service in this 1947 photo. Key points on the blackboard include "Report promptly for work 8 a.m. (in uniform)." Under the section on appearance, classes emphasized neatness and cleanliness while prohibiting "dirty socks, hair flowers, chewing gum, and ear rings." The section titled "Be quiet" earned a heading all its own. Above: One-on-one training followed group instruction in 1947, with special lessons on the gentle art of the pillowcase. Photos by Reni Newsphoto Service.

and Patrisha Frazier, followed her into the hotel kitchen where they prepared food. Stated Adele in an interview at the time, "As long as my daughter and granddaughter have good, decent, honest jobs, I love to have them working with me."

In story after story from employees past and present, what emerges is their universal passion for and pride in

The Mayflower and the place in history she represents. Weathering Allan Walker's financial demise in the very beginning, the Depression, misguided modernization, even labor disputes, The Mayflower has never closed her doors, due in part to the commitment of her crew.

Throughout the years hotel management has proven equally devoted. Even during the extensive renovations in the 1980s when as much as half of the hotel was closed off at times, the hotel relocated employees to other departments rather than lay them off during the restoration. Although a unionized property, they have a work-and-walk philosophy. During rare strikes, they work their shift and then walk a picket line, rather than cripple the hotel's service, states Frank Fleming, a night auditor, who, with thirty-six years at The Mayflower, is yet another devoted member of her extended family. Wayne S. Carney, the hotel's newest director of finance, states, "In my years of working, I've never worked with union hotels before, yet the staff here is outstanding. With employees here, their job comes first."

That commitment must not have been easy at times. In 1963, the back of the house was still segregated, with separate locker rooms and cafeterias labeled "white" and "colored." But by the late 1960s, Mayflower management

Thirteen of the thirty-five senior staff pictured here in 1940 were part of the original 1925 crew of The Mayflower.

had implemented training and diversity programs that set the tone for the nation. In keeping with President Lyndon B. Johnson's right-to-work program, Hotel Corporation of America launched a nationwide push to hire and train the "Chronically Unemployed," stated the headline in the June 1968 issue of *Inn-Side HCA*. HCA President Roger P. Sonnabend had announced the program at their May stockholder meeting. HCA, at the time, was owner of The Mayflower. The twelve-month program would recruit and train professionals in all areas of hotel industry and management.

The Mayflower also embraced another program by the National Alliance of Businessmen to employ blacks and minorities: In February 1969, another *Inn-Side HCA* article authored by program member and Mayflower employee Toni Waiters stated that, "On November 18, 1968, the NAB (National Alliance of Businessmen) program went into effect at The Mayflower. I am proud to be part of this program," Waiters wrote. "Through NAB, we are trying to understand ourselves in order to understand our work and the community. We are building stronger backgrounds in Math, English, Minority History, and have a special class entitled World of Work to make us aware of the rewards of working rather than being unemployed," Waiters emphasized. At the time of the article, The Mayflower had placed seventeen trainees throughout the hotel staff, including Toni Waiters.

What endures at The Mayflower is a standard of service that transcends time, color or class distinction in either her staff or the guests they serve. Human resource director Sara Moore explained, "We put a committee in place to create awareness and appreciation of the differences and uniqueness of all our different cultures. The committee— C.A.R.E., for Committed to Appreciating and Respecting Everyone—just did a survey and surfaced over seventy different countries. Then we contacted a flag company to get

1968

Astronaut James A. Lovell is guest of honor at the YWCA Luncheon in the Grand Ballroom October 7th.

as many flags as we could from all those countries." At a recent associates meeting, she described the scene when everyone came walking in with their flags: "It was very powerful. It helps explain why two people might not look at the world or the cafeteria menu or days off the same way."

Diversity is "not just about the associates and heart of the house," Moore continued. "It's very representative of what's happening out there with guests as well. We serve people from those same seventy languages and countries. Maybe more so." In the interview in October 2000, Moore underscored her point with yet another history-making event taking place at the hotel. "We have the delegation from North Korea this week. They haven't been to this country in more than fifty-five years. What kinds of foods, customs, protocol do we need

Mayflower maitre d'hotel Fred Wiesinger (right) and Chef Nicholas Marchitelli attend to one of the lavish banquet tables prior to a 1948 feast. Fred, known universally by just his first name, had been with the hotel since its opening and Marchitelli was part of the brigade du Mayflower by as early as 1929. Before coming to The Mayflower, Fred had served the Hapsburgs of Austria. Photo by Reni Newsphoto Service.

to know? Every week at The Mayflower, we've got some VIP we're trying to understand how best to serve."

Jimme Curtis, who started as a coffee boy in the Presidential Room December 27, 1957, says his most memorable moment was not waiting on Eleanor Roosevelt. Nor was it meeting Barbara Jordan (D-Texas 1973–1979), the first black woman elected to Congress from the South and the first woman keynote speaker at the Democratic National Convention in 1976. A shy man, Jimme thought back and said the event that has meant the most was the day thirty years ago "when they asked me to be a waiter." He remembers, "I felt good. It was a compliment, the opportunity they offered me." Now a banquet servant, Curtis says, "It's the kindness and respect of the ownership of the hotel and the work. I love meeting people and trying to make people happy in my service. I'm proud to be working in The Mayflower. I wouldn't ask for anything greater on the face of this earth than being able to work at this hotel, and that's the God's truth."

Although it presented formidable obstacles from a construction standpoint, The Mayflower would emerge from soil infused with that same sense of unselfish service much like that provided by the sisters of the Convent of the Visitation for almost fifty years. From its beginning, The Mayflower's "heart of the house" has set a standard of loyalty and dedication not found in any other hotel. Theirs is truly a labor of love.

Chef de cuisine Nicholas Marchitelli, center, inspects the delicacies waiting in refrigeration for the moment when the silver platters will be carried to the buffet table for what was obviously an important event in this 1950s photo. With him are Night Chef Tony Macerollo, left, who would succeed Marchitelli as chef de cuisine, and a Chef Maruzzo. Notice the enormous cuts of meat hanging in the background. Remembers one employee, "The butcher shop was even larger then . . . a real butcher shop. They would buy half a cow, entire pigs, lamb and veal. They made their own ground beef." The hotel was self-contained in other ways as well, such as its own news department. The dateline on this photo reads "News Bureau, The Mayflower, Washington 6, D.C., news chief, Bab Lincoln." Photo by Reni Newsphoto Service.

1969

Coach Vince Lombardi sets up housekeeping in Suite 675 as he begins his tenure as executive vice president of the Washington Redskins.

Employees reaching the twenty-five-year mark along with The Mayflower in this 1950 photo included James Brown, lobby houseman (front left); Hattie Williams, housekeeping (third from left); Bonnie Knight, chief phone operator (fourth from right), and Sidney Seidenman, bandleader and musician (far right). The back row included Chef Nicholas Marchitelli and, to his left, C.J. Mack, who would remain with The Mayflower for more than thirty years, the majority of that as manager. Photo by Reni Newsphoto Service.

Anthony Macerollo, right, a Mayflower chef for more than thirty years, surveys the giant cake made for the anniversary of the Louisville Slugger bat makers. The occasion was the 1958 meeting of the top major and minor league baseball players at The Mayflower. On one typical morning in 1962, "Tony" prepared breakfast for 2,000 that included President Kennedy, Vice President Johnson, members of the Cabinet and numerous other representatives of The Hill and Diplomatic Corps. Just days later, he was feeding the guests at a buffet hosted by Morocco's new ambassador, Ali Bengelloun. Photo by Reni Newsphoto Service.

Above: General Cashier Robert Alderson handled money in a big way. In his 39 years, 2 months, 5 days of service, Robert Alderson would hold positions as inventory clerk, coffee shop manager, payroll analysis, service manager, security and finally general cashier, his difficult but most rewarding. In an interview at his retirement in 1985, he recalled that in the old days only the hotel's general manager was paid by check. All other employees were paid in cash and as general cashier, it was his job to deliver. Photo courtesy of Willie Gordon.

As he was in this late 1950s photo of The Mayflower's exclusive location on Connecticut Avenue, rain or shine, Mike Mann was always at his post during his forty-two years as doorman. Photo courtesy of Frank Fleming.

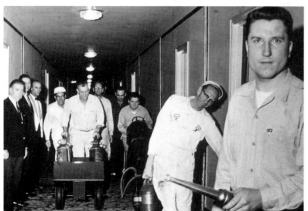

The Mayflower's fire brigade goes through a fire drill in this mid-1960s photo. At far right is Anton "Tony" Lamplot who came to work at the hotel on March 3, 1963. Lamplot now is one of the senior staff in Engineering. He remembers when groceries were delivered to the permanent suites. "There was an outside door to each apartment and the groceries were put there. The guests opened a separate door inside to get the delivery." Tony remembers one resident in particular: "Supreme Court Judge Reed lived here for 10 years. He was almost 90 when they moved the permanent residents out."

For almost three-quarters of a century, The Mayflower handled all its own laundering with a staff of fourteen employees who worked feverishly to keep the hundreds of rooms supplied with clean linen. In this circa 1960s photo, the linen service staff feed an average of twelve sheets per minute into the gigantic presser. In 1998, The Mayflower decided take-out and delivery service would be more efficient and cost effective and the equipment was removed. Photo by Reni Newsphoto Service.

Oyster shucker Thomas A. Gaskins had been with The Mayflower twenty-two years in this 1965 photo. With him is another Mayflower veteran, Wei Hong Woo, who was in charge of the Chinese kitchen. Photo by Reni Newsphoto Service.

The Mayflower's gift to the Christmas season for many years was a giant gingerbread house, which was presented to the children at St. Ann's Infant Home on New Year's Eve. The masterpiece pictured here weighed some 80 pounds and featured marzipan figures of Hansel, Gretel, the Witch and St. Nicholas. Five hundred mint shingles covered the roof and more than three hundred gingerbread logs fenced the three-foot-high confection. Planned and executed by Maitre Patissier Manfred Prim, right, this 1964 completely edible creation earned Prim the Artistic Individual Masterpiece Award from the Fifth Salon of Culinary Art sponsored by the Washington Epicurean Club and the Restaurant Association. At left is Chef de Cuisine Anthony Macerollo. The man in center is James Nassikas, food and beverage manager of the hotel at the time.

At its fortieth anniversary, the hotel brought out its famous gold service—by now reserved for only the most special guests—to honor all employees at The Mayflower with more than twenty-five years of service. The head table, though, was reserved for seven employees who had been with the hotel since it opened. Here they are shown centered around the cake made by the hotel's kitchen especially for the event. Pictured clockwise from top left are: Bonnie Knight, chief phone operator; George Gaskins, window washer; Mike Mann, doorman; bottom row, Hattie Williams, housekeeping; Sidney Seidenman, bandleader; Wyvon W. King, superintendent of service; and James Brown, lobby houseman. Not shown was C. J. Mack, who was also a Mayflower "plank owner" (a nautical term referring to a member of a ship's inaugural crew). According to the article that accompanied the photo, "Vice President Hubert H. Humphrey paid a surprise visit to the 40th anniversary dinner and referred to The Mayflower as 'my second home' and said that he 'feels like an adopted member of the hotel.' President Johnson sent an autographed photo to Mr. Mack in honor of the occasion, and former President Truman wired, 'I'll be with you in spirit as you celebrate this milestone.'" Photo from Hotel Corporation of America News, April 1965; courtesy of Frank Fleming.

"Night Time is the Right Time" is the caption night auditor Frank Fleming, second from left, placed on this 1979 photograph from his scrapbook. With him, left to right, are fellow night auditors David Harris, Lee Tanksley, Arif Khan, and Bruce "Fast Fingers" Frink, whom the January 1979 Mayflower's Log cited as "Department of the Month," for their ability to "post with the speed of lightning, leap piles of machine tape in a single bound, produce a revenue report while answering phones, play mail clerk while registering a guest." Says Fleming of this alternative work schedule: "The city is sleeping but we're wide awake. Who else takes their 'morning shower' at 10 o'clock in the evening, their lunch break at 3 o'clock in the morning. We're here to put the house to bed, posting charges and totaling bills. But as we go home in the morning there is a feeling of satisfaction that while everyone else is starting their day, we'll be in a deep slumber. So when you see us punch out in the morning, just smile and say 'Good night.' We'll understand." Photo courtesy of Frank Fleming.

These were the scenes behind the front desk before computers on January 18, 1979. Messages and mail are slotted by hand in hundreds of mail bins while, in the second photo, desk clerk Bippy Bijai processes a guest using old fashioned pen and ink. The "buckets" behind him to the right held registration information. The foreign currency exchange rates posted provide an interesting economic snapshot. Courtesy of Frank Fleming.

Doorman Earl Smith models one of the brand-new uniforms that were all the rage in 1979. Notice the Connecticut Avenue storefronts at the time. Courtesy of Frank Fleming.

A small console now replaces the extensive board in the telephone room, shown here in 1979. Pneumatic tubes connecting to the front desk, housekeeping and the main restaurant could carry messages or even keys. Courtesy of Frank Fleming.

Senior banquet captain Vicente G. Gonzalez, of Quito, Ecuador, planned to stay in the United States only six months after his arrival to visit relatives on September 8, 1956. He has been here ever since, most of that time with The Mayflower. He is pictured here circa 1979. As described in other chapters, Vicente's Mayflower window on the world has allowed him to witness some of the most historic events in the nation's history. Photo courtesy of Frank Fleming.

Part of the hotel's old guard, Eddie Derendorf, left, and Bob Beavers see to yet another guest's arrival. Derendorf and fellow doorman Al Dobbins became such celebrities at the hotel that in November 1998 they were featured on "Oprah Winfrey." According to current Bell Captain Joseph Brackeen, Beavers' uniform dress was part of a ritual each morning. Described Brackeen, "His shirts were tailored, his shoes always shined, rain or shine. He would cock his hat just a bit to the right." Photo courtesy of Frank Fleming.

The Mayflower's engineers take a break in the employee cafeteria, aptly named The Galley by Louis Holly who won the naming contest in the 1970s. Photo courtesy of Frank Fleming.

Between them, these three Mayflower doormen would accumulate more than 120 years of service in "the front of the house" before they retired. They are, left to right: Bob Beavers, Mike Mann and Lonnie Suiter. In this 1965 photo, Mike Mann, one of The Mayflower's original employees, shows off the gold watch he received for his fortieth year. Mike's hobby was playing the stock market, a passion he shared with his buddy, wealthy financier J. P. Morgan, who was a regular guest. Another friend of his—J. Edgar Hoover—helped Mann obtain his U.S. citizenship. Beavers and Suiter retired in 1999. Photo by Reni Newsphoto Service.

Employees at this 1980 awards banquet in the Grand Ballroom shared roast beef and Baked Alaska, music from the '30s and '40s and a slide presentation of days gone by. Bellman Dominic "Jocko" Tutela, seated left front, was rather short and had a special baggage cart with a lower rail for hanging bags. Photo courtesy of Frank Fleming.

1970

The National Association of Bank Women holds the largest convention to date at The Mayflower September 20–24.

At one of the hotel's recent functions honoring long-term employees, Frank Glaine and his bride Beverly, right, are pictured with Jessie Smail, director of Convention Services and a lifelong friend of the Glaines. The February 1969 Inn-Side HCA, a trade publication featuring innkeeper news, related this fairytale: "Once upon a time, in October 1952, Frank Glaine came to work at The Mayflower as a mail clerk. He noticed a pretty girl named Beverly who was working in room reservations. Frank asked Beverly to lunch, and before long, asked her to marry him." Married almost 17 years at the time of the article, Frank was banquet coordinator and Beverly worked as catering sales representative. Beverly retired in 1993 after 47 years of service; Frank had also served the hotel for more than 45 years when he retired. Sadly, death proved the only thing that could separate them when Beverly died of cancer in March 2000. Their legacy, however, remains. It was Frank who first hired George DeKornfeld, still cited by the staff as one of its most beloved managers. Although DeKornfeld could speak no English, having newly arrived in the United States in 1951 after fleeing the Communists in Hungary, Frank hired him to work in the mailroom. Armed with his passionate belief that "America is still the land of opportunity" if you "just concentrate a little more and work a little harder," DeKornfeld became The Mayflower's general manager in 1976. Photo courtesy of Jessie Smail.

On April 11, 1977, Walter Seligmann, second from right, is toasted by Mayflower General Manager George DeKornfeld, right, on Farragut Square, two blocks from The Mayflower. The occasion was Seligmann's sixty-fifth birthday and impending retirement after forty years at the hotel in the banqueting department. During the party, Seligmann "reminisced about dinners for heads of state at the hotel and the evening when waiters were dismissed and he alone served a small gathering as then-President Eisenhower briefed them on classified subjects," according to an article in the next day's Style section of the Washington Post. "I've gone through seven general managers, eight food and beverage managers and four different corporations at the Mayflower," he said at the time, "and they never told me to leave. I guess I did okay." Also wishing Seligmann well at his party were veteran Mayflower employees Beverly Glaine and Jessie Smail, to the right of the candelabra. Photo courtesy of Jessie Smail.

The original caption for this 1978 photo reads: "The Food Storeroom on the kitchen level has the qualities of a neighborhood grocery store and gourmet shop all rolled into one. The man in charge, Willie Gordon, has to hustle to keep it organized and serve his 'customers' (our cooks) quickly. Willie's been at it quite awhile and he's got an eye for quality as well. As Willie says, 'if it ain't fresh . . . I'm outta business!!'" Willie retired July 5, 2000, after more than forty-three years. Photo courtesy of Willie Gordon.

In this 1979 photo, The Mayflower's executive chef, Bernard Binon (right), and White House chef Henry Haller, examine some of the 1,100 pounds of meat being prepared by the hotel for the 1,400 guests at the historic Menachem Begin–Anwar Sadat dinner March 26. The White House kitchen had been requested to prepare a state dinner for that many people to commemorate the signing of the peace treaty between Egypt and Israel. But because of work space limitations, and very short lead time, outside help was needed. So Chef Haller contacted his old friend and colleague, Chef Binon. Following a hastily called conference with the hotel's management and his staff, Binon accepted the assignment. While the world watched the historic peace treaty signing, Chef Binon and his staff of renowned chefs—Arthur Gant, David Lassale and Wilbert Williams—went to work. By 5 p.m. that evening, the trays of cooked meat and tubs of sauce were packed into an insulated truck and sped to the White House, along with its chefs and food and beverage director Jurgen Dinger and executive steward Steve Sekula, all of whom assisted with serving and seating guests from around the world. A letter of thanks from the White House read: "Although most of the guests were not aware of it, the dinner would not have been possible without the outstanding cooperation and assistance of the Mayflower staff to the success of this historic event." Photo by Mattox, courtesy of Frank Fleming.

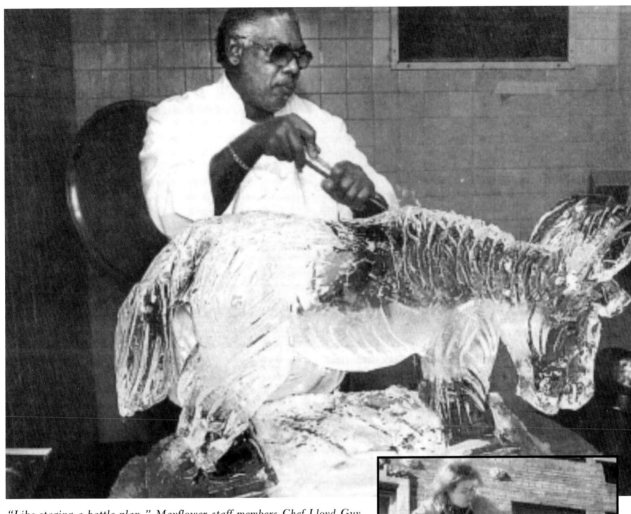

"Like staging a battle plan," Mayflower staff members Chef Lloyd Guy (top) and Lori Ann Johnson, a floral decorator, are shown preparing for guests and festivities scheduled for the presidential inaugural in this January 17, 1997, article from the Washington Times.

This article from the Washington Post *featured a special Mayflower guest on hand for Take Your Daughter to Work Day. At left is Tameka Able, granddaughter of Alberta Collins who has worked in the engineering department for nearly forty years. Photo by Michael Williamson, article courtesy of Alberta Collins.*

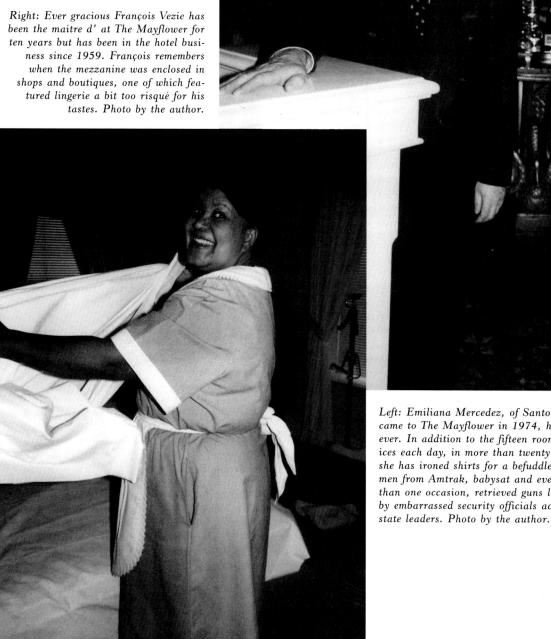

1973

Gerald Ford is offered the position of vice president at a summit meeting in the Chinese Room following the resignation of Spiro T. Agnew.

Right: Ever gracious François Vezie has been the maitre d' at The Mayflower for ten years but has been in the hotel business since 1959. François remembers when the mezzanine was enclosed in shops and boutiques, one of which featured lingerie a bit too risqué for his tastes. Photo by the author.

Left: Emiliana Mercedez, of Santo Domingo, came to The Mayflower in 1974, her first job ever. In addition to the fifteen rooms she services each day, in more than twenty-five years, she has ironed shirts for a befuddled businessmen from Amtrak, babysat and even, on more than one occasion, retrieved guns left behind by embarrassed security officials accompanying state leaders. Photo by the author.

Sam Serves Magic with Spirit

Called "the Alan Greenspan of the capital's bar scene" by the *Washington Post* for his ability to predict elections based on drink preferences, Sambonn Lek, head bartender for the Mayflower's Town & Country Lounge, has served the rich and infamous there for twenty-four years. It is not the "spirits" he serves that seem to lift folks' spirits, however.

One day many years ago, Sam watched as someone in the bar performed a simple magic trick. He was struck by the reaction of those watching. "Their eyes lit up," he remembers. Clumsy in the beginning, Sam began amassing his own magic tricks one by one. "I did a sloppy job at first," he admits, "but people relax. They forget about their problems. They think about me instead of trouble at home."

Eventually Sam's tricks became legendary and a fan club developed. Hundreds of letters began filling the pages of his scrapbook. Senders ranged from Erica, Peter and Betsy Cohn; Conte and Contessa Ferri de Lazara of Venice; Albert J. Pinder, publisher for the Grinnell, Iowa, *Herald-Register*; to even the ambassador from Cambodia, Roland Eng. The one Sam likes most is the painstakingly printed note from a sad little patron: "Dear Sam, before I met you I was feeling really down. You made me feel great. Thanks for saving my 8th Birthday for me. Your new friend, Katherine Talmadge."

In response to all his fan mail, and at his own expense, Sam began sending out Christmas cards each year as a gesture of good will. "Maybe it was fifteen cards at first, then thirty, then a hundred, then seven hundred," he recalls. Now at least two thousand of his special friends receive the personally designed cards each year. Sam has made such a name for the hotel, however, that it now picks up the tab for the cards and the postage, although Sam still does the addressing. "If you show honesty and loyalty to the hotel and make money for them because the guests come back, then that goodwill comes back to you.

The more you give, the more you get," he believes.

Grateful to a land that gave him a home when his native Cambodia fell to the Communists, Sam became a citizen in 1980. He never forgot his homeland, though, and in recent years he has gone back to give of himself in other ways, to do charity work there. Looking away, seeing in his mind those mean streets that once were his home, he says quietly, "It broke my heart to see all the poor people there." In Sam's 2000 visit to Cambodia, he brought rice, medicine, clothes, school supplies and eyeglasses to 330 people. "Next year," he vows, "my goal is more than one thousand."

Sam never forgets bartending, the craft that allowed him to make a good life for his wife and family. He works as hard perfecting new drinks as he does perfecting new magic tricks. His very own creations include the "Mayflower Royale" made with vodka, vermouth and Chambord, and Uncle "Sam I Am" made with Absolut citron, cranberry juice and amaretto; "State of the Onion" gimlet martini. But it is not the spirits he serves that make him so many friends. It is the magic, the thousands of Christmas cards, the gift of his own gentle spirit that calms people down when they enter the place where Sambonn Lek holds court.

Sambonn Lek, pictured on the cover of one of his famed Christmas cards, lifts spirits as well as he serves them in The Mayflower's Town & Country Lounge. Photo courtesy of Sambonn Lek.

SAMBONN LEK'S MAYFLOWER ROYALE

3 oz. Belvedere vodka
Dash of dry vermouth
A drip of Chambord
After pouring mixed drink into chilled
martini glass, top with twist of lemon.

A House Divided

At any major hotel there are two worlds. The "front of the house" is that near façade of serene elegance that puts forward the hotel's best faces—the appointments of the hotel's public spaces and guest rooms, and the staff who work them. In marked contrast, step behind one of the doors in The Mayflower marked "Staff Only" and you enter a bustling beehive of hundreds of workers hurrying in single-minded mission to serve their queen. Behind those doors are narrow stone steps hollowed by thousands, perhaps millions of footsteps that have worn away the stone as they scurried to serve.

This parallel world has been known in hotel code as the "back of the house." In a gesture of respect to its unusually loyal associates, Mayflower management prefers to call its cadre of professionals "the heart of the house." Regardless of the reference, it is a place as strangely remarkable as the one Alice entered through the looking glass. While only steps away, it is worlds apart from the image of unhurried elegance it creates. Not only do you step into another world but almost another dimension, for it is the "back of the house" that bears the patina polished

by thousands of hands and decades of service. Here, as in some mighty castle, miles of unadorned corridors and uncarpeted elevators lead to gleaming-clean service areas where steam rises from mighty cauldrons, where sauces simmer from scratch, where pastries rise in vast ovens, where, by hand, fruits are still carved and cakes transformed into giant, sweet confections.

As the example in this timeless art of service, through the years The Mayflower has opened its doors as a classroom for hotel management. One awestruck neophyte was Lottie N. Werden, a student in Class 2–45 of the Lewis Hotel Training School in November 1945. While a few of the services described are no longer performed in-house, the level of service and attention to detail endure. What Lottie captured in her four-page, painstakingly typewritten paper not only earned her an A+, in these excerpts she also provides a vivid account, as timeless as if it had been written yesterday, of The Mayflower's "back of the house:"

At 3:00 O'Clock, [we] met Mrs. Eckert in the lobby of the Hotel Mayflower. We were conducted on a tour of the Back of the House by Asst. Mgr. Mr. Graves. . . . It was a very busy place, bell boys were paging and yet very

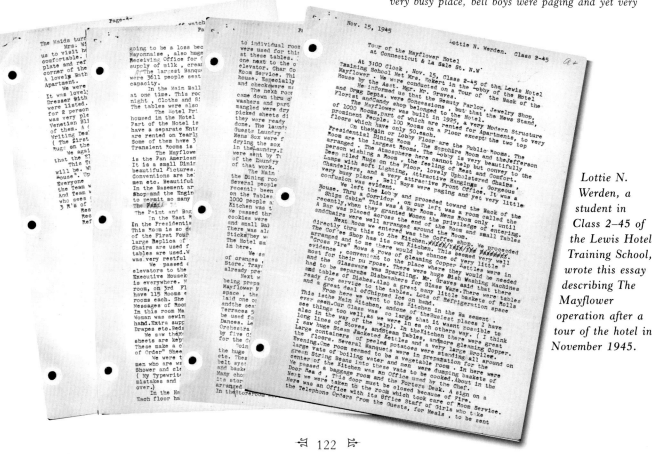

Lottie N. Werden, a student in Class 2–45 of the Lewis Hotel Training School, wrote this essay describing The Mayflower operation after a tour of the hotel in November 1945.

Chef Nicholas Marchitelli, center, grills his staff as they prepare a holiday banquet in this 1937 photo. Notice the narrow steps to the right in the photo, behind the chef peeking around the corner. The stone steps remain, worn and indented now by perhaps millions of trips by food service staff.

little confusion was evident. We left the lobby and proceeded toward the Back of the House . . . to the kitchen in the basement. This is the main kitchen, and one of the busiest places I have ever seen. There were great long lines of stoves, and steam tables, and more gleaming copper. I saw huge steam jacketed kettles and a very large broiler. Large containers of peeled potatoes were standing all around on the floors. . . . One room seemed to be a vegetable room. In here were large vats of boiling water and men were dumping baskets of green string beans into these vats to be cooked.

The Main Kitchen was connected thru passageways to all the dining rooms. We passed thru the Pastry & Bake Shops. At this time little cookies were being made in the Bake Shop. In the Bakery, rolls and small baking powder biscuits were being worked with.

We saw the huge dishwashing machines. Oh so many dishes, wine glasss, etc. These dishes reached the dishwashers by means of an endless belt system.

We saw the Storeroom, with its stock on hand. Crates of oranges, cartons of other things, bananas, melons, apples, avocados, kegs of mayonnaise. In the corridors were stacked 100# bags of potatoes and baskets of string beans. Like a small Grocery Store. Trays & trays of delecious [sic] looking fruit cups were already prepared. In the fruit cups . . . were beautifully arranged grape fruit & orange segments, melon balls and cherries. We went thru the Butcher Shop. Many chopping blocks were in use. We saw the Wine Room, with its store of goods.

Next we were taken to the room which took care of Room Service. Here was an office with its office staff of girls who take the telephone orders from the guests, for meals, to be sent to individual rooms. Small drop leaf tables with white cloths were used for this service. These tables were taken to rooms by elevator. Char Coal Heaters [sic] were used to keep food hot

for Room Service. This is the most profitable service in the house. Especially for Breakfast.

The next room we visited was the Laundry. Soiled clothes came down thru chutes. These were sorted and run thru the washers and partially dried, then run thru manglers and when mangled were dry enough to be placed in storage. Girls picked sheets directly off the mangler and folded them and they were ready for use again. Here some mending was also being done. The laundry of workers uniforms was also done here. Guest laundry too was done. A half dozen forms for drying mens sox were fastened on a table. This was used for hurridly [sic] drying the sox of men guests. There were between 60 & 70 people in the Laundry. Packages were sent by tube for delivery.

Next we were taken to the Sapphire Room. This room was being prepared for a banquet. The tables were laid with white Mayflower monogramed linen and silver. In the Presidential Dining Room is the head waiter's desk. This room is so called because of the large oil portraits of the first four presidents, hanging on the wall. Here is also a large replica of the Ship Mayflower. Beautiful tapestry-covered chairs are used for seating guests.

We again went to the Lobby by Elevator, and I noticed that the Elevator Operator made perfect landings.

This tour gave me a very good insight into what hotel life will be. When in the "Back of the House" I thot [sic], "What a Mad House." Upon thinking more about it, I came to this conclusion. Everyone filling his own position to the best of his ability, the team work of all the people, and team work of every department, is what gives to the guest, who sees only the Front Office at work, the feeling of the 3 R's of hotel work. Rest. Recreation. Refreshment.

Captains of The Mayflower

For the first few decades after opening, The Mayflower was not only owned but also operated by those who held her title. The Walker Hotel Corporation owned the emerging edifice from 1922 to 1924. Just months before opening, due to massive construction cost overruns, Walker was forced to sell controlling interest to C. C. Mitchell who was an officer in the American Bond & Mortgage Company, one of Walker's major financial backers. Mitchell and his partners in the Mayflower Hotel Corporation would both own and manage the hotel from 1924 to 1946.

It was not to be smooth sailing for these owners either. Caught like other investors in the financial disaster of the Great Depression, the holding company was forced into court-appointed receivership in 1931 but rescued in June 1934 by the Roosevelt Administration's Corporate Reorganization Act.

Twelve years later, on December 29, 1946, Conrad Hilton and his Hilton Hotel Corporation bought The Mayflower for a mere $2.6 million, a fraction of what it had cost to build. Hilton's formula for acquisitions contained five points: (1) the hotel must be well built, (2) soundly financed,

(3) strategically located, (4) of real value to its community, and (5) reasonably well managed. At $2.6 million, The Mayflower was a real bargain. The minority stockholders of the Mayflower Corporation challenged the low sale price because they felt they had been forced to accept an unfairly low price, but the U.S. Court of Appeals upheld the sale. In 1956, after being found in violation of antitrust charges that he was monopolizing convention business in several cities, including Washington, Hilton was forced to sell some of his properties, including The Mayflower.

After ten years under the ownership and management of the Hilton Hotel Corporation, the A. M. Sonnabend Family of Boston purchased The Mayflower in March 1956 for $12.8 million, still not much more than what the hotel had cost to build thirty-one years before. Like professional sports teams, owners are not necessarily managers of their own properties. The Sonnabend agent for the hotel's management was the Hotel Corporation of America, later Sonesta International Hotels.

In 1966, four men with Washington roots, like Walker, would take The Mayflower on as a labor of love. Ulysses Auger, Dominic Antonelli, William Cohen,

Henry L. Merry, president of the Mayflower when it opened in 1925, "came to Washington in the early autumn of 1924, under urgent pressure from the hotel owners, to undertake the seemingly impossible task of completing the then unfinished structure,—decorating, furnishing and equipping it, and organizing the personnel in time to stage here the Presidential Inaugural Ball of 1925," stated the March 1927 Log. *His original intention was to remain only long enough to launch the huge project, but he was induced to remain in active management of the operation during the uncertain days of its infancy. Two years later, after seeing The Mayflower take its place as one of the outstanding hotels of the country, he left to "probably seek other hotel worlds to conquer." A* Log *editorial lavished praise on this first Mayflower captain and described the*

crew's reaction to his leaving:

The Mayflower staff, as a mark of their affection and an indication of their grief at his departure, presented him with an antique grandfather's clock. The little manifesto accompanying the gift voiced the feelings of the entire organization: "Because we love him; because we admire the greatness of his accomplishment in so successfully launching The Mayflower and so skillfully piloting her through the early stages of her life's voyage; because we respect the dignity and fairness of his administration, and appreciate the effort he has consistently made to bring happiness and contentment to each of us in our respective fields of work, we, the crew of the old ship—present to our beloved Skipper this slight token of our deep affection."

By 1927, still under forty years of age, Daniel J. O'Brien, president of the Mayflower Hotel Company and the hotel's general manager, was already "widely recognized as one of the foremost authorities on hotel accountancy," noted the October 1927 Log. Entering the hotel business in New York City almost two decades before, O'Brien had gone "by leaps and bounds from one promotion to another." Emphasizing the enormous growth in the hotel industry, the Log reporter wrote: "It is a far cry from the modest, low-pitched tavern of by-gone days to the sky-scraping hotels of the present era. And it is a far cry, too, from the A.B.C. kind of accountancy that the old-time Boniface used in keeping the finance records of his simple establishment to the vast machinery that has to be employed to solve the stupendous and complicated problems that now confront the management of the larger modern hotels." Based on his success, O'Brien was persuaded to co-author with Charles B. Couchman, a fellow American Institute Accountant, a book published by McGraw-Hill entitled Hotel Administration—Accounts and Control. Doomed not to be a bestseller by both its title and subject, it nonetheless received "extremely favorable reviews" and was credited with, for the first time in hotel history, bringing together in a "systematic whole, accounting records and methods that have been tried and found successful." Photo by Harris & Ewing.

and Kingdon Gould Jr. formed May-Wash Associates and bought The Mayflower from the Sonnabend Family for only $14 million. They would eventually embark on one of the most significant private commitments to preservation in Washington. (See Chapter 6.)

Under May-Wash ownership, holders of the hotel's management contract would be Hotel Corporation of America until 1971; Westin Hotels until 1981; and finally Stouffer Hotels. According to author Judith Cohen, "Stouffer decided to make The Mayflower the flagship of its growing hotel business. This decision was not without a personal element: The Stouffer Hotels president was now William Hulett, the man who had been general manager of the Mayflower in the early 1970s. He knew from direct experience what promise the hotel held, and what was needed to realize that promise." Not only did Stouffer assume management; in 1982 they also became partners with May-Wash, purchasing 12.5 percent interest in The Mayflower.

For several years, these partners and their management companies chartered a new course for The Mayflower, one that restored her reputation as Washington's premier hotel. Some time after a formal reopening November 20, 1984, following completion of renovations, the May-Wash partners decided it was time to let go, selling their interest to the Nestlé Company, Switzerland, who had assumed own-

ership of Stouffer. Nestlé now became sole owners of The Mayflower and would own as well as manage the property until 1993.

Apparently wanting to concentrate on the food business, Nestlé sold The Mayflower, along with the entire Stouffer chain of hotels, to the Cheng Family of New World Development, Hong Kong. The Cheng Family also owned other luxury properties worldwide under the name Renaissance Hotels. To help establish the Renaissance brand, for a time they retained the Stouffer name for advertising purposes. Thus the hotel became The Stouffer Renaissance Mayflower Hotel until the late 1990s.

Although still owned by the Cheng Family under C.T.F. Holdings, in 1997 Marriott took over the management contract. While the Renaissance name remains on the letterhead, it is now a subtitle. The Mayflower name and embossed ship logo are once again the singular symbols of her endurance as a national landmark.

Judging by the ongoing investment in The Mayflower's appearance, amenities and reputation, both the Cheng Family and its Marriott agents seem equally committed to the hotel's preservation and status as "Washington's second best address."

1974

President Richard M. Nixon holds a farewell reception for his staff at the hotel prior to announcing his resignation; Gerald Ford becomes president.

Mayflower Managing Director C. J. Mack hoists the Hilton flag denoting the acquisition of the hotel by Conrad Hilton in 1946. The tall gentleman in the bellman's uniform, center, is longtime Mayflower employee Pete Flaherty. Third from right is Aubrey Brown. Photo by Ankers Photographers, courtesy of Frank Fleming.

GENERAL MANAGERS

1925–1929
Henry L. Merry, President
Daniel J. O'Brien, General Manager
Arthur J. Harnett, Resident Manager

1929–1941
Ralph L. Pollio, General Manager

1941–1965
C. J. Mack, General Manager/Managing Director

1965–1971
C. J. Mack, Managing Director
John Craver, General Manager

1971
Ed Checkijian, Transition General Manager (Sonesta to Westin)

1971–1973
Michael Lambert, General Manager

1973–1974
William N. Hulett, General Manager

1974–1976
Robert B. Wilhelm, General Manager

1976–1979
George DeKornfeld, General Manager

1979–1981
Gerald Wolsborn, General Manager

1981
Steve Harper, Transition General Manager (Westin to Stouffer)

1981–1984
Eric Ewoldt, General Manager

1984–1992
Bernard Awenenti, General Manager

1992–1994
Anthony Stewart-Moore, General Manager

1994–1999
Jim Biggar, General Manager (through Stouffer to Renaissance)

1999–Present
George J. Cook Jr, General Manager (Renaissance Hotels, one of Marriott's brands)

Right: Every six months, in April and October, investors in the Mayflower Hotel Company would cash in maturing coupons for a $30 dividend on their hotel stock. Caught like other investors in the financial disaster of the Great Depression, The Mayflower Hotel Company was forced into court-appointed receivership in 1931, rendering investments like this 1928 $1,000 bond at 6 percent interest nearly worthless.

Below: A special train—The Hilton Special—bore Mayflower owner Conrad Nicholson Hilton and his guests to Washington for the hotel's silver anniversary February 21, 1950. Hilton is pictured eighth from the left. Corneal John "C.J." Mack, Mayflower general manager, is fourth from left. In addition to the "Hiltonites," more than fifty "hotel men" from such other luminary establishments as The Greenbrier, West Virginia; The Waldorf-Astoria, New York (a Hilton property today); and The Plaza, also in New York, attended the anniversary reception. These professionals hosted more than two hundred guests "of rank," such as half the foreign ambassadors and ministers in Washington, every U.S. military secretary, and enough senators and congressman to nearly form a majority vote, including Senator and Mrs. Lyndon Baines Johnson. Photo by Reni Newsphoto Service.

Nicholas Sabatini
ROYAL CHEF

While its stunning architecture and unprecedented amenities got the most press during The Mayflower's string of successful opening events, one key "ingredient" almost lost to history was initially one of the hotel's crown jewels. According to his obituary in the *New York Times* when he died in 1936 at age fifty-five, Nicholas Sabatini, was an internationally known and much-honored chef who spent most of his career serving the aristocracy. Lured from New York's old Hotel Delmonico by Mayflower manager Henry Leroy Merry to the position of executive chef, Sabatini began his career at "Quirinale," the royal Italian residence, on the occasion of the silver anniversary of King Umberto and Queen Margherita when he was recruited by his father, also a great chef, to help with the royal event. After this apprenticeship at the palace, he served in hotels in Paris, London, Cairo and Lucerne. In St. Petersburg, Russia, he entered the service of Princess Cantacuzene.

This notation, written by Sabatini's daughter Rina Sabatini Conway, appears in a scrapbook she compiled on her father: "Nicholas Sabatini worked at old Delmonico Hotel, New York. When it closed, he was persuaded to come work for the new Mayflower hotel in Washington by Henry Leroy Merry. Mr. Merry was a very good family friend. (My younger brother is named Henry Leroy after him.)" The notation further indicates that Sabatini decided not to uproot his family from New York, "commuting back and forth to our home in Brooklyn, New York, every weekend for about 4 years (1929), then went back to the new Delmonico, on to Ambassador until his death in 1936," wrote his daughter.

Sabatini's culinary contributions and accomplish-

NICHOLAS SABATINI'S CHICKEN TETRAZZINI

5 tablespoons butter
2 tablespoons flour
1½ cups chicken stock
1 dash cayenne pepper

1 dash nutmeg
Salt and pepper to taste
2½ cups boiled, sliced chicken

½ pound mushrooms
Butter for sautéing
⅓ cup white wine
1 cup heavy cream

In large saucepan, melt 4 tablespoons of butter. Stirring briskly, add the flour and continue stirring for several minutes without letting the mixture brown. Add the stock, cayenne and nutmeg, and season to taste with salt and pepper. Reduce the heat slightly and let cook, stirring occasionally, while sautéing the chicken and mushrooms in a separate pan.

Add the chicken and mushrooms, wine and heavy cream to the butter and stock mixture and continue cooking—without boiling—for 4 or 5 minutes (the sauce should be good and hot).

Cook the spaghetti to *al dente* according to the instructions on the package (or, if fresh, for 2 to 3 minutes).

Drain the spaghetti and place it around the edges of a buttered, 2-inch deep backing dish. Fill the center with the chicken and mushroom mixture, and pour the last bit of sauce over the spaghetti. Sprinkle Parmesan atop the ingredients, dot with a tablespoon of butter, and place in a 375-degree oven until the sauce begins to bubble and the cheese is golden brown. Serve immediately. Makes 8 servings.

This priceless late 1920s photo of The Mayflower's original celebrated brigade and management also captures in one scene some of the hotel's most notable features: the replica of the Mayflower at center; the columns within columns, ornamental plasterwork, and ornate balustrades of the famed Grand Ballroom; and most prominently, its first executive chef, Nicholas Sabatini, seated appropriately on the throne-like chair in the center. To his left is Mayflower manager Henry Leroy Merry (in suit), who lured the great chef from his "reign of kings," a phrase from the New York Italian newspaper, Il Progresso, which ran his obituary August 19, 1936. It was for Nicholas Sabatini that The Mayflower's famed Nicholas Restaurant would be named in the 1980s. Photo courtesy of Rina Sabatini Conway.

ments, unfortunately, were almost forgotten, eclipsed by another Chef Nicholas—one Nicholas Marchitelli—whose tenure at the hotel lasted more than thirty years, obscuring the memory of the first Chef Nicholas. Explains Rina Conway, "Marchitelli was from the same little village, Villa Santa Maria, as my father, who brought him to the Mayflower." Nicknamed "Village of Chefs," the tiny village achieved such fame because of its world-renowned chefs—Sabatini and his father, as well as Marchitelli—it opened its own international school for chefs, the "Istituto Professionale." Rina proudly emphasizes that it was for her father, not the later-day Nicholas as indicated in an earlier Mayflower history, The Mayflower's popular Nicholas Restaurant, which operated into the mid-1990s, was named.

It was at New York's Delmonico where Sabatini cooked up his greatest legacy, Chicken Tetrazzini. Sabatini created and named the dish—still served on occasion at The Mayflower—for Eva and Louisa Tetrazzini, famous Italian opera stars in the early 1900s. Made in the U.S.A., this now famous "Italian" dish was the main course at a White House luncheon for Italian leaders given by President and Mrs. Dwight D. Eisenhower September 30, 1959, stated an October 1, 1959 article in the *Washington Post*.

The Music Men of The Mayflower

Mr. Sidney Jr., son of The Mayflower's most beloved bandleader, began roaming its halls at only two years old. His best friend was Larry Wiesinger, son of Fred Wiesinger, The Mayflower's first maitre d'hotel. His father, Sidney Seidenman, signed on for what became his extended, thirty-year engagement at the hotel in 1926. He led as many as nine orchestras playing up to eight hundred bookings a year.

By 1929, nothing less than Sidney (he was better known by his first name) and his orchestra would do for presidents and debutantes and the dinner dances of diplomats. "To the debutante set there is but one appointed orchestra—'Sidney'—and no debutante can properly make her bow unless he and his cohorts are doing the musical formalities. To the Washington bud a debut without Sidney is like an automobile without wheels," stated a 1930 review.

One engagement became a command performance. During Christmas week in 1929, an emissary from the White House called on Sidney and informed him that the President and Mrs. Hoover wanted him to play at their son Allan's New Year's Eve party. "For orchestras as well

Bandleader and violinist "Mr. Sidney," as he was best known, memorized the favorite tunes of the hotel's special guests. He is pictured here in the 1930s. Photo courtesy of Sidney Seidenman Jr.

as guests, White House requests are commands," wrote one account of the event, and Mr. Sidney wielded the baton as his band played jazz at the first "whoopee party" ever held there.

Sometimes the presidents engaged him on his own turf. President Harry Truman joined him at the piano for "The Fairy Waltz" and "Chopsticks." President Eisenhower loved to sing along when the band played "I've Got Spurs That Jingle, Jangle, Jingle." He prided himself on granting special requests. Eccentric Mayflower resident Evie Robert hired him and the orchestra to celebrate the birthday of her horse, John the Baptist. Music to accompany silent movies were one early specialty and even after he signed on at The Mayflower, Washington socialite Evelyn Walsh McLean "had Sidney bring a 12-piece orchestra to her town house to provide music for the silent movie she

Washington grande dame Marjorie Post, right, "was one of my dad's best accounts," recalls Sidney Seidenman Jr. Photo by City News Bureau, courtesy of Sidney Seidenman Jr.

Summer Tunes by Koons

DICK KOONS
Leader
of Sidney's
Singing Band

in the delightfully
Air Conditioned
Meeting Place
which flourishes
the year 'round

★

DANCING

Afternoons after 5
Evenings after 10

★

MAYFLOWER
LOUNGE

*"Summer Tunes by Koons" was the headliner in The
Mayflower Lounge in the 1940s. Dick Koons was the
leader of Sidney's Singing Band, one of as many as nine
bands which played up to eight hundred engagements a
year under the supervision of Sidney Seidenman Sr.*

invariably showed after supper," wrote *Washington Star*
staff writer Richard Slusser. "President and Mrs.
Harding seldom missed one of McLean's Sunday
evening soirees," the paper reported.

It was his father and their shared love of music that
gave Sidney Jr. hope as he fought in Europe during
World War II. "I was one of 15 out of 180 men in my
company who wasn't either killed or wounded," he
remembers. "I lived only to come back home to The
Mayflower and take up music again." Unlike his father,
who was a violinist, Sidney Jr.'s forté was piano. After
graduating with a bachelor's degree in music, he went
to work as business manager for his father's orchestra.
Between them the father and son serenaded
Washington's elite for half a century.

Although no longer performing there nightly,
"Sidney's Music & Entertainment" still provides the
music for countless Washington engagements, from big
band to bagpipes and everything in between. One of
their performers, Danny Ruskin, brother to satirist
Mark Russell, has performed at the Mayflower's Town
& Country for twenty years. The address for Sidney's
Music is still 1127 Connecticut Avenue NW, same as
The Mayflower, although Sidney and his partner,
Robert J. Dodelin Jr., now also operate out of another
office nearby. Like his father before him, Sidney Jr.
still gives special engagements, serenading a lone inter-
viewer at the end of a delightful meal.

━━◈═━━

*Like his father before him, Sidney Jr. (pic-
tured below) and his partner Robert J.
Dodelin Jr. still provide music for countless
Washington engagements. Photo courtesy of
Sidney Seidenman Jr.*

Norman Wade

A CHEF FROM THE HEART

Chef Norman Wade apprenticed with the Café Royale in Picadilly. He catered for 10 Downing Street in London, and served as chef tournant at the Paris Plaza Athenée. His international culinary awards would fill several scrapbooks. A handwritten note from Vincent Price telling him how much the famous actor enjoyed meeting Wade and "having a chance to sample your art" lies tucked away in a loose-leaf binder. A snapshot of Wade sparring with Mohammed Ali is temporarily misplaced somewhere at home. And his clam chowder concoction won the Boston Chowderfest so many times that, to even the playing field, organizers had to eliminate him from the competition by inducting him and his recipe into the Chowder Hall of Fame.

Yet the only obvious adornment in Mayflower Executive Chef Norman Wade's office in the heart of the cavernous kitchen is a time-faded copy of a book by perhaps the greatest chef of all time: Auguste Escoffiér. It sits propped at an angle, the cover image of Escoffiér staring back as if from a treasured family photo. With the single-minded focus of a marathon runner with his eye on the finish line, Wade's passion is his art. Everything else falls away.

In fact, Wade is a marathon runner who finished several times in the Boston event during his tenure there as executive chef at The Westin Hotel, Copley Place.

Out of his element, Chef Wade spars with Mohammed Ali when the Greatest Athlete of All Time was guest speaker at The Mayflower on a forum for Parkinson's disease.

Soft-spoken, ever vigilant, during an interview his eyes scan the pots and grills and work surfaces through his windowed office as his staff of forty-two prepares a marathon of meals for the thousands who will feast that day in the Café Promenade, the Town & Country Lounge, through room service, at banquets, not to mention the six hundred employees who will be offered two different entrees in the Galley, The Mayflower's staff cafeteria.

While an interview reveals his background—born in Newcastle, England, introduced to cooking at age 16 by his uncle who got him his job at the Café Royale—only the tour of his domain reveals the essence of this man. Like the copper pots simmering with stock, distilling to clear broth the ingredients that are his secret for the most delicious soups and sauces, everything but Norman Wade's passion for his creative craft falls away. "Everything must be fresh, the vegetables, the fruits, the fish, no bouillon, nothing frozen."

His parting advice to other aspiring cooks is the key at last to this great chef: "Cooking comes from the heart. You have to really enjoy doing it." In the end, as it was at first glance, the simple image of his hero Escoffiér is fitting testament to the talent and achievements of this uncharacteristically self-effacing master chef, Norman Wade.

Executive chef Norman Wade, right, and a member of his staff take a quick photo break during The Mayflower's 75th Anniversary Celebration in March 2000, when the hotel herself was the guest of honor amidst the other seven hundred or so guests. Photo by the author.

NORMAN WADE'S CLAM CHOWDER

6 Quahaug clams
10 Cherrystone clams
1 medium onion, diced
1 stalk celery, diced
1 large potato, peeled, diced,
    and blanched

40 oz. clam juice
1 pt. heavy cream
1 clove garlic, minced

4 oz. butter, clarified
1/2 tsp. white pepper
1 small bay leaf
1 cup water
1/4 tsp. thyme
white flour

Wash clams thoroughly. Place Quahaugs and 1/2 cup water in soup pot, cover tightly, and steam until clams open. Remove, chop coarsely, and reserve, also reserving broth.

In soup pot, add clarified butter and garlic. Sauté 2-3 minutes. Add onion, celery and spices. Sauté until onions are translucent. Add flour to make roux, stirring constantly. Cook over low heat for 5 minutes (don't brown). Slowly add clam juice, stirring constantly to avoid lumps. Simmer for 10 minutes. (The soup will be very thick, so be careful it doesn't burn.) Add potato and cook until tender. Add cream and clams and bring back to boil. Season to taste.

Fathers, Sons Share Zest for Cooking

"You should become a chef so you will never starve," Cesare Buggio urged his son Agostino "Tino" when he was growing up in Dijon, France. While not a professional chef, the senior Buggio—who ran a tile and construction business—"was a chef at home," remembers Tino. "My mom cooked lunch, my dad cooked dinner." The smell of great food filled the house when Tino came home from school, and on Sunday he watched as his father took great pleasure in feeding their guests.

Tino's mom remembers that his first foray into the kitchen at age 13 was to prepare a big batch of tomato sauce. In what was perhaps a sign of things to come, the young chef stirred up a cauldron of sauce big enough to feed "about 500 people," Tino recalls. By age 14, when most boys are still batting balls, he had entered the Hyppolite Fontaine College in Dijon, and by 17 he had landed a position at the Hotel de Paris in Monte Carlo where he prepared meals for Prince Rainier, Princess Grace and the royal family.

Born in Italy, raised and trained in France, hired as chef tournant at La Mere Michel Restaurant in Montreal, Canada, Chef Buggio's cuisine is a deliciously eclectic blend from a variety of countries, including Norway, Denmark, Italy, France, Portugal, Spain and, of course, the United States. He has shared his secrets with thousands through PBS, FOX, ABC and NBC, who have filmed him

Mayflower executive sous chef Agostino "Tino" Buggio, right, pauses for a toast with his friend and photographer, Len de Pas, at the hotel's 75th birthday celebration in March 2000. Photo by Mattox.

AGOSTINO BUGGIO'S POLENTA CRABCAKES

4 oz. polenta (Italian cornmeal)	1 oz. unsalted butter
1 1/2 cups chicken stock	2 oz. grated Parmesan cheese
1 lb. jumbo lump crabmeat	1 tsp. Angostura (aromatic bitter)
1 tsp. virgin olive oil	1/2 tsp. Tabasco
2 whole eggs	1 tsp. Worcestershire sauce
1 shallot	Salt and pepper to taste

Bring chicken stock and olive oil to a boil; allow to boil for 20 minutes. Add polenta and stir constantly with a wire whisk or wooden spoon for 5 minutes. Set aside. Melt butter and sauté one finely chopped shallot. Add crabmeat, Worcestershire sauce, Tabasco, Angostura, salt and pepper. Remove from heat. Add polenta mixture. Mix thoroughly. Add two whole eggs and Parmesan cheese. Shape into two-inch round cakes and set aside. Heat 1 tbsp. olive oil in a pan. Cook crabmeat for 3 minutes, browning each side. Serve.

in his element at The Mayflower. Most recently, he placed second in the finalrounds of the Pierre Taittinger competition in Paris, where he represented the entire United States. The Mayflower credits Buggio, its executive sous chef, with maintaining its AAA Four Diamond status since he arrived in 1986 to manage The Mayflower's Nicholas Restaurant (named for Nicholas Sabatini, the first Mayflower chef) where Buggio was proud to personally serve such celebrities as Kirk Douglas, Peter Jennings and Cokie Roberts. While the specialty restaurant closed in the mid-1990s, Chef Buggio's superb Mediterranean cuisine is prepared daily in the immensely popular Café Promenade restaurant. Tino served his tasty morsels to Sophia Loren, Charlton Heston, Bob Barker and Wayne Gretsky, in 1999–2000, some of the more recognizable faces in the Café, where everyone is served as a celebrity. Tino also oversees the popular power lunch in the Town & Country.

Buggio reserves the most pride for his 17-year-old son Vincent, who inherited his father's and grandfather's flair for food. In a 1995 interview with the *Washington Post*, Buggio stated, "When Vincent was smaller, 5 or 6 years old, he used to stand on a chair in the kitchen and stir the sauce. At home he makes his own dough for pizza." Like his father, who claims fish are his specialty—such as turbot from Europe, Dover sole, and American rock fish—Vincent is equally particular about his fish dishes. "The only time Vincent will eat whole fish is when he catches it." Fortunately, father and son go on regular fishing trips together. Like father, like son, like son, Cesare, Tino and Vincent share a love of fine food that spans the continents and a love for each other that has leavened the bond between these three generations of talented chefs.

Nicholas Restaurant, which opened in 1984, routinely received rave reviews for its atmosphere and cuisine, overseen by Chef Agostino Buggio. Though dining trends took patrons away from specialty restaurants and Nicholas closed in the mid-1990s, fortunately Chef Buggio's cuisine remains in the Café Promenade.

The walls of today's Chinese Room, once red as pictured in this late 1980s photo, are now white. However little else has changed, despite numerous makeovers throughout the hotel's 75-year reign.

CHAPTER 5

Art and Architecture
The History Behind the History

*"Truly, wanderers that we were upon the face of the earth,
we felt ourselves home at last and gave thanks to the Lord
that this, our country to be, seemed so fertile
and promising a land for habitation."*

—Log of the Mayflower, *by Philip J. Simon*

The early 1900s were "a time of great optimism," writes architectural historian Christopher Weeks. "Clients wanted and would pay for the best, and art was respectable enough to set at the table when the money was being served. Not only were prominent architects of the period . . . given important commissions in the capital, but their buildings were embellished by the work of sculptors such as [Augustus] Saint-Gaudens, Daniel Chester French, and Lorado Taft."

At its opening, so much "respectable" art adorned The Mayflower's public spaces that it competed with guests for not only attention but also floor space, as shown in an early picture of the Promenade. Within months, a 1925 advertising brochure written by Capital Advertising Associates would read:

Rooftree of a thousand restful rooms, this unequaled institution inevitably becomes the Mecca toward which the pilgrims of the world turn their faces. . . .

On the main floor is the Presidential Restaurant, its walls decorated with the official seals of the various States.

In the approach to the ballrooms, and, as part of the exquisitely appointed Promenade, the Palm Court—a space beautiful as the fabled hanging gardens of Babylon—challenges instant attention. The Promenade, a stretch of colonnaded gallery, offers a vista a tenth of a mile long and is constantly alive with a moving throng, gay with the variegated colors of many modish costumes—sport and formal dress of the women, uniforms and civilian clothes of the men.

A glimpse to the right of the Promenade discloses a magnificent ballroom on the main floor with mezzanine balconies fitted with handsomely appointed boxes, and with a well-proportioned stage designed for concert use or for small theatricals.

Never before in the history of Washington, D.C., had there been such a place as The Mayflower's Grand Ballroom, "the most opulent space in the hotel," as it has been labeled by architectural historians. Rising to the full height of the mezzanine, the enormous rectangular room is flanked by two narrow, double galleries enclosed by wrought-iron balustrades as intricate as that in the mezzanine, with winged female torsos and fruit-filled urns. Massive piers, nearly every inch covered by intricately designed low-relief decorations trimmed in gold leaf, divide the ballroom into three major bays. Smaller piers, also dripping with detail and topped with gilt capitals of exquisitely rendered satanic faces, define three sub-bays.

One contemporary description of the hotel states that its "walls, floors, stairs, pilasters and wainscoting . . . are clad in a wide array of American and imported marbles," no less than ten different varieties. Examples of the beautiful blending of these expansive treatments still abound in the Grand Ballroom, where balustrades on the lower floor rest on curved monolithic bases of black-and-gold Italian marble. A wainscot of golden tan St. Genevieve marble surrounds the room and six sets of raised-panel doors opening from the

1976

April 5th Swedish-American
Conference at The Mayflower
is attended by King Carl Gustav
of Sweden.

Promenade give guests easy access down steps of the same material. More of the St. Genevieve marble graces the Café Promenade, where walls of Caen stone and floors of Biesanz American Travertine completed the original Palm Court. Marbles from U.S. shores grace the East and State Rooms, where white Alabama and Vermont marbles accented with Verde Antique and Italian Pavonzizzo trim the walls and flooring. As it did on opening day, Botticino marble lines the semicircular alcove across from the elevators that now houses the concierge desk.

The Mayflower's suites, with bedrooms more luxuriously furnished than any other hotel bedrooms in the world," according to the 1925 brochure, received similar attention to detail. Two palatial suites—the Presidential and Vice Presidential Suites—occupied the entire ninth and tenth floors of a million-dollar annex completed shortly after the hotel opened. "[M]arvels of reposeful elegance and charm," a 1925 brochure noted that the interior decoration, including not only art but also furniture, draperies, even floor coverings, "were done by artists of worldwide reputation. . . ." The state rooms, like Beresford's clarion description of them, were perhaps a bit overstated:

This early photo records the elaborate features of the original main entrance on Connecticut Avenue, most of which remain today. The original marquee still hangs suspended by metal rods anchored by lion's head anchor brackets. The alternating arches and oval windows created an optical illusion that obscures the visual differentiation between the first floor and mezzanine levels. Large limestone medallions, with carvings of roses, ribbons and wheat sheaves surrounding a lion's head drip from the roof line. The Mayflower Pharmacy at left closed long ago and the doorway is now the outside access to The Town & Country Lounge, but the oval window crowned with a woman's head and festooned garlands remains. Photo by Dunbar-Stewart Photos.

In this photo of the richly decorated original Promenade, art competed with guests for floor space in the expanse which, to this day, extends one-tenth of a mile across an entire city block. Both of the two original Mayflower paintings hang on the right wall, although only the larger one depicting the landing can be distinguished. Beautifully restored, it still hangs in the Promenade, although farther down. The other painting, to the left, shows the Mayflower under sail. It is one of two now hanging behind the registration desk. Farther down the Promenade's wall are the two seventeenth-century Aubusson tapestries still on display there today. An appraisal in the 1930s described the cloisonné vase on the octagonal table in the foreground as from the eighteenth or early nineteenth century and belonging to the collection of famed actress Sarah Bernhardt. It now sits in an alcove at the entrance to the Café Promenade (inset). The lovely large marble statue with its winged back to the camera, left in center, is "La Sirène," one of three statues by Denys Puech visible in the picture. "La Sirène," along with "Merope," and "Flora," were sold in 1948 to the National Memorial Park in Falls Church, Virginia. At the opposite end of the expanse appear to be wrought-iron doors, perhaps installed to insure the privacy of the permanent residents whose entrance was located at De Sales Street nearest the 17th Street entrance. A comparison of the chandeliers pictured would suggest that most of the original lead crystal embellishments were incorporated into those hanging today. Photo by Tenschert, courtesy of Frank Fleming; inset photo by the author.

Nothing to equal them is to be found anywhere in Europe or the Western Continent. Each a suite of thirteen rooms planned and equipped for permanent residence with drawing-room, dining-room, library office, five guest rooms each with private bath and glass-enclosed shower with silver fittings, kitchen and servants' rooms, they are as luxurious as any Old World palace, together with all the modern conveniences inseparable from American ideals of comfort. With their Oriental rugs, tables, consoles and cabinets of painted lacquer and marquetry, chairs upholstered in hand-woven tapestries and satin damasks, crystal, cloisonné and bronze and marble objects of art, original oils and engravings on the walls, satin and taffeta hangings to carry out the color harmonies, these are rooms indeed fit for the royal and other distinguished guests of the nation for whose entertainment they are designed.

Artists of a different sort took care of both guests' and hotel management's every need. "For as long as forty years after the hotel opened, it was self-sufficient," states Anton Lamplot, who has been with the hotel since 1963. "Everything was made here. We made all our own ice in the C1 level—block ice, crushed ice, cubed ice. The bakery shop worked all night and made any kind of bread, bagels, doughnuts. We made our own ice cream. There

Mythical creatures dance around the dome of the Chinese Room in this photo (top) taken January 24, 1928. The occasion was a dinner in honor of William T. Cosgrave, president of the Irish Free State, hence the shamrock-shaped banquet table. The choice of the allegorical figures to decorate the dome is a mystery; however, photos contained in Washington Post archives refer to it as the "Chimera Room." In Greek mythology, a "chimera" was a fire-breathing female monster with a lion's head, a goat's body, and a serpent's tail, or any fabulous beast with parts taken from various animals. While it may have been the intent of the designers to call this room "Chimera," the name was most likely too obscure to endure, and from the outset it was dubbed the "Chinese Room." The name would prove portentous, for throughout its history The Mayflower has been the site of numerous summits and stays by Chinese leaders. Most notable was the eight-month occupation by the Chinese delegation while they awaited refurbishment of their two Embassy Row buildings nearby following diplomatic mission exchanges with the United States in 1973. Apparently the Chinese Room's embellishments were not enough, for at times it underwent such fantastical transformations as that pictured in the gypsy-like scene (inset) not long after the hotel opened. Miraculously, the room has endured basically intact and the chinoiserie paintings of people, trees and animals still dance around the dramatic elliptical dome. Photos by Schutz.

was a venetian blind and upholstery shop. At the valet shop, guests could have their pants pressed right away."

The Mayflower sailed through both the Depression and World War II with its elegant appointments virtually untouched. But nothing had prepared it for the bulldozer known as Conrad Hilton. Hilton purchased controlling interest in the hotel in 1946 for the paltry price of only $2.6 million and ordered sweeping changes that would drastically alter the authenticity that had been The Mayflower's signature symbol.

The original Mayflower Garden was located directly below the lobby level where, "On an elevated plateau surrounding the dance floor are tables for the service of tea, dinner and supper, a delightful rendezvous for all informal affairs," according to the April 1926 Mayflower's Log. Lanterns hung from latticed arbors and crossed latticed beams between which were murals painted to represent the evening sky. "Although the room is in reality well below the street level under the main lobby floor," wrote Mayflower designer Robert Beresford, "the entire atmosphere of the garden is suggestive of the open air."

Wrote Mayflower chronicler Judith Cohen, Hilton "set about remodeling The Mayflower to appeal to vacationing families and to the growing convention business," two categories of customers who were on the move in the prosperous postwar years. Cohen describes the carnage:

The gold leaf in the Ballroom, the brocade curtains, the silk-upholstered furniture, and period furnishings—none of these old-world touches seemed right to Conrad Hilton. Nor was the art-gallery look of the Promenade, with its fine cloisonné and tapestries woven by old masters of Aubusson. The Promenade's three main sculptures were sold to National Memorial Park Cemetery in Falls Church, Virginia. The gold leaf, so lauded in the hotel's opening years, was covered over with paint. . . . It was as if an elegant ocean liner had been converted into a no-frills ferryboat.

Once-faithful customers expressed their silent screams of protest by staying away in droves, and Hilton got their message. His next renovation effort a scant three years later and coinciding with The Mayflower's twenty-fifth anniversary was more carefully considered. The Lounge was redone in Georgian style. Warm rose shades replaced the shades of gray that were supposed to have given the room a modern appearance with the first renovation.

1977

Following President Jimmy Carter's warning that the U.S. energy crisis could bring on a "national catastrophe," the *Mayflower's Log* begins running energy saving reminders, such as the hotel's electric bill for May: $37,272.

Comfortable furnishings once again welcomed forgiving patrons, prompting Washington columnist Harry MacArthur to write: "Conrad Hilton . . . can come back now. All is forgiven. Veteran inhabitants of The Mayflower who snarled bitterly when Mr. Hilton went to vast expense to undecorate their favorite rendezvous a couple of years ago, can have nothing but high regard for him today."

Not even the concessions of Conrad Hilton himself could stop the flight and blight that would plague downtown D.C. in the sixties. By then, the Mayflower's sails had started to droop. Her gilt tarnished, the prisms and crystal of her elegant chandeliers cracked or lost, her spectacular skylights still covered from World War II, The Mayflower was losing its fashionable image. A changing economy made it difficult for many tourists to afford The Mayflower's first-class accommodations. Those guests who could afford the best booked at newer, flashier establishments.

The Mayflower had lost its distinction in other ways as well. Hilton's first makeover removed much of the ornamental plasterwork on the walls and ceilings. Another major "upgrade" in 1961–62 covered up nearly all The Mayflower's assets in the public areas. Vinyl brocade hid the rough plaster walls in the Promenade. But the most striking change was in the mezzanine. Pseudo-wood paneling boarded up the mezzanine's beautiful wrought iron railings and gold capitals. Camped around the mezzanine were offices and shops, instead of the once-inviting alcoves featuring elegant, intimate seating areas that induced moments of reflection or quiet conversation. A dropped acoustical ceiling not only blocked the skylight but also visually and aesthetically diminished the entrance that had once lavishly greeted guests with marble columns rising two stories to the richly embellished ceiling.

As was the case with the misguided modernization of the Mayflower Lounge, the Sapphire Room, with the "mystical Star Sapphire stone" as its inspiration, was another design disaster. The September 1940 Mayflower's Log *contained the only reference found to the opening of this public space—formerly The Mayflower Garden (pictured on previous page)—below the main lobby, where "modern principles" were used in both lighting and décor. "Sparkling glass blocks and aluminum surfaces contrasted against the dominant blue produce a spirited effect without loss of mellowness or intimacy," stated the* Log. *As shown in this rendering, "unnecessary ornaments have been eliminated in favor of broad, plain areas," a sterile scene that also apparently eliminated guests. The* Log, *in a curious footnote to the announcement, stated that K. Gordon Merrill, a director and member of the Executive Committee of the Mayflower Hotel Corporation, conceived the design, while Robert F. Beresford (not Warren & Wetmore), "original architect of The Mayflower, who has likewise participated in every structural change and decorative revision since the founding of the hotel," carried out the work. Restored and renamed as the Colonial Room, the space today is a room "of superior design" and "an attractive example of the Colonial Revival decorative trend that swept the country after World War II," records the document that nominated the hotel for historic designation. Although below ground level, artificial lighting slanting in through louvered doors-to-nowhere cast a glow as if of sunlight in much the same effect as the hotel's famous skylights.*

The renovations that reinvented The Mayflower nearly every decade consigned some of its original masterworks, including not only paintings, statues, and rare furniture but also china, giant silver serving pieces, even great chandeliers to closets, storerooms and basements of the hotel where they were forgotten. Some were lost or destroyed. Others were so damaged, defaced or broken that their value was obscured, and they were either carted away or landed in the trash. An article in the *Washington Post* confirmed that at least three of the large marble statues originally on display in the Promenade—"La Sirène," "Merope," and "Flora"—were sold in 1948 to the National Memorial Park in Falls Church, Virginia, where, as of 1983, they remained.

Miraculously, much of the hotel's patrician architecture and priceless art survived the no less than six major renovations in the hotel's history that dramatically altered not only the public spaces but also the original guest rooms and private apartments. The nomination of the hotel to the National Register of Historic Places states that "the wealth of surviving original material adds significantly to the historical and architectural interest of the hotel."

The restoration that would once again unmask many of The Mayflower's architectural assets would also uncover buried treasure lost for decades. Workers discovered packed away in a long-locked basement storeroom valuable gold, silver and cloisonné serving and centerpieces, urns, vases and candelabra worth several thousand dollars each. Additional finds were two large New Deal era murals by renowned Works Progress Administration muralist Edward Laning. Located in the Café Promenade, the murals had been boarded up during a misguided modernization in the early 1960s.

The Mayflower pioneered in such amenities as a remarkable air cooling system, running ice water, a central vacuum system and bathrooms in every guest room including servant's rooms. The range of The Mayflower's guest facilities, the level of its service and its advanced mechanical systems have set standards by which the world's best hotels have been judged for three-quarters of a century. Highly innovative in 1925, all are commonplace today. What cannot be matched is the unique blend of art and architecture that have become The Mayflower's hallmark. Luxuriously appointed in the best tradition of Beaux Arts eclecticism with fine French, English and American antiques when it opened, The Mayflower had once rivaled the stately castles of Europe. While some of

> ## 1979
> The Mayflower prepares the state dinner honoring the Arab-Israeli Peace Treaty signing held at the White House.

these appointments have been lost, a wealth of the original treasures remains to embellish what has been termed by contemporary architects as "the chaste elegance" of The Mayflower's suites and public rooms. Hotel architect Whitney Warren once stated that "great buildings give dignity to people's lives," and he had great reverence for things that were old. It is a reverence fortunately shared by those initially responsible for finishing and furnishing Allan Walker's dream, by those who would lead the restoration, and by the hotel's contemporary caretakers, vigilant preservers of The Mayflower's historic art and architecture who recognize that her past is the key to her future.

Just fifteen years old in this 1940 photo, the lobby and Promenade still glisten. The sentiment under an almost identical photo that appeared in an ad placed by Bigelow Weavers, New York, in the February 1940 Mayflower's Log *"Salutes The Mayflower on its 15th Anniversary of success and importance in Washington life!" The ad reads, "The magnificent Mayflower lobby is carpeted with Bigelow Austrian loom tufted rugs," and notes, "For fifteen years the Mayflower has dispensed hospitality to high-ranking executives in our national government, to diplomats, to a host of visitors in our Capital. Bigelow . . . reflects with pride that throughout these successful years its famous rooms have been Bigelow Carpeted." Photo courtesy of Frank Fleming.*

Right: The Empire Suite, pictured here in 1932, comprised "one of the finest collections of Louis XVI furniture and other unusual French pieces that were the property of Marie Antoinette," according to the February 1932 Mayflower's Log. Photo by Underwood & Underwood.

Below: This 1930s photo by Harris & Ewing of an apartment entrance attests to the elaborate appointments afforded guests.

The apartment lobby entrance, shown here circa 1948, was reached from De Sales Street, away from the main lobby opening on Connecticut, to afford permanent residents the utmost privacy. The original revolving doors pictured led inside to a reception desk and a set of elevators exclusively for apartment residents. Photo by Reni Newsphoto Service, courtesy of Frank Fleming.

Above: Its beaming skylight painted over, the lobby appears dim and foreboding in this World War II-era photo. The hotel abided by blackout rules for the duration of the war. Unfortunately, it was not until over forty years later that the blackened skylight once again let in the sun to brighten the public spaces below. Photo by Blakeslee-Lane.

The Promenade had been uncluttered in this 1948 photo by Blakeslee-Lane.

This view from the main elevator lobby looking toward 17th Street shows the sunken level of the Promenade as it appeared in 1948. The use of these varied levels throughout the public spaces—there are five on the ground floor alone—give guests a vista as they approach different rooms and are one aspect of the hotel's architectural charm. Photo by Blakeslee-Lane.

The fifth floor elevator lobby had been modernized and stripped of the old-world elegance that had been the hotel's hallmark in this late 1940s photo by Blakeslee-Lane. This was called the Dorothy Draper Floor after the designer who gave it a modern style different from all the other floors.

The Mayflower
Washington, D. C.

INTER-OFFICE CORRESPONDENCE

FROM   Mr. Cook
TO   Mr. Roberts   May 10, 1941
SUBJECT ROOM SERVICE MENUS

The housekeeping department reports that our Morning Glory menus have been taken away by guests in such quantities that more are required at once. Is an inside printing of five hundred okay immediately, or is an increase in food prices contemplated soon, which would make a temporary delay preferable?

The Mayflower's own mint julep, at only $.78, was one of the "warm weather suggestions" on this room service menu in 1941. The menus themselves were such popular souvenirs that an emergency printing became necessary. Stated a May 10, 1941, memo, "The housekeeping department reports that our Morning Glory menus have been taken away by guests in such quantities that more are required at once."

As guest of honor at The Mayflower's twenty-fifth anniversary party February 21, 1950, Conrad Nicholson Hilton, second from left, president of Hilton Hotels, cuts the massive cake adorned with a replica of the hotel. With him are, left, Colonel Henry Crown, vice president of Hilton Hotels; Thomas C. Clark, Associate Justice of the U.S. Supreme Court, second from right; and Corneal John "C.J." Mack, Mayflower general manager. After Hilton purchased controlling interest in the hotel in 1946, he ordered sweeping changes that for a time drastically altered the authenticity of The Mayflower. The conspicuous absence of its once faithful patrons let Hilton know loud and clear that they disapproved of these "modernizations," and at least some of the elegance of the hotel's public spaces was restored in time for the twenty-fifth anniversary celebration.

Three of the elaborate gilt and polychrome state crests that line the walls of the East and State Rooms stand out clearly in this photo showing the room in ready for an event in the 1950s. This area, across the Promenade from the present Café Promenade, was the Presidential Restaurant when the hotel opened in 1925.

Pictured at a 1953 Democratic fund-raiser in the Chinese Room, President Harry Truman preferred the confines of The Mayflower to those of the White House and spent a tremendous amount of time here. "For reasons no one quite understands," according to hotel lore, Truman nicknamed the fruit-laden serving piece in front of him the "Cherubs of Tivoli" and apparently developed a particular fondness for it. Whenever possible, the piece was used on his head tables. It is on display today in the Café Promenade. Photo by Reni Newsphoto Service.

President Dwight D. Eisenhower was among the crowds who came to the National Capital Flower & Garden Show in 1955. The Mayflower's gold service set off the orchids in this display arranged by the hotel's own florists to such advantage that it took first prize in its category of cut flowers for its exhibitor, Thomas Young Orchids of Bound Brook, New Jersey. Photo by Ankers Photographers.

The Mayflower's signature logo adorned the bedspreads in less elegant rooms in this 1957 photo by Blakeslee-Lane.

1983

The Mayflower is entered in the
National Register of Historic Places.

A Place to Shine

Opening in 1925 and located below the lobby reached from stairs inside the main entrance, to the left, The Mayflower's Boot Black is Washington's longest operating shoeshine stand. Its first patron—and the source of its nickname—was Vice President-elect Charles Dawes who instructed the attendant on duty to, "Make those boots black, my good man!" An itinerary of the vice president-elect's activities of that day that ran in Washington's evening papers began with "a shoe buff at BOOT BLACK Shoe Shine at the new Mayflower Hotel." The name replaced the intended "Mayflower Shoe Shine," and both the nickname "Boot Black" and the service have endured for 75 years. Current manager James "Jimmy" Miler provides the same spit-and-polish service as his father and uncle did at The Mayflower long before he was born.

The busiest day for Boot Black occurred March 3, 1933, the day before Franklin D. Roosevelt's Inaugural Ball at the Mayflower, when shiners polished over 1,500 pairs of shoes. Douglas Fairbanks Jr. holds the record for a single individual seeking the service: wanting to keep his options open for an evening reception at the White House, he sent out seventeen pairs of shoes for shining in 1945. Proclaimed the Best Shoe Shine by *Washingtonian Magazine*, Boot Black may also have gone the farthest in creative service. Arriving late to speak at an industry dinner,

the chief executive officer of a major international corporation realized he had left the bag containing his dress shoes on the airplane. Boot Black immediately went to work on the only shoes he had with him—a pair of white golf shoes. In a matter of minutes they removed the tassels and spikes and transformed the snow white shoes into a pair of elegant jet black wing tips. Telltale black smudges on The Mayflower's marble floors were the only evidence of the transformation.

The post-card pictured here relates the story of the day actor Rex Harrison misplaced his soles after he placed them outside his room, an English custom not done in America. But Mayflower service prevailed. A hotel associate had delivered the shoes to the bootblack shop where they were found, shined and ready.

The day The Mayflower saved Rex Harrison's sole.

The ultimate Englishman was staying in one of our suites. And that night he put a pair of shoes out in the hall for the bootblack to polish. It was a perfectly logical thing for an Englishman to do, since it's customary in European hotels for the bootblack to make the rounds of the corridors at night. But it just isn't done in most American hotels.

The next morning, Harrison got up quite early and discovered that not only were his shoes not shined—they were missing. He told the staff, and the Manager on duty, afraid that the shoes had been stolen, wrote out a check for them immediately.

But he also played a hunch. And checked with the bootblack's shop in the hotel. Sure enough, Harrison's shoes had been brought in the night before. They'd been polished. The only reason they hadn't been replaced outside his door was that no one expected a movie star to rise quite that early.

To this day, nobody at The Mayflower knows who acted above and beyond the call of duty. It might have been a chambermaid or a room service waiter or bellman. But it really doesn't matter. Someone was concerned enough to figure out what those shoes were doing in the hall and take a moment for an extra bit of service.

So the next time you need special service, try us. We don't always do things strictly by the book.

REX HARRISON
MAY 1945

HISTORY IN THE MAKING

The Mayflower

During a major renovation in 1947, attempts were made to modernize the hotel, including removal of much of the ornamental plasterwork on the walls and ceilings of what was the Palm Court, now the Café Promenade. Fortunately, in other public areas, renovators merely boarded up the ornate plaster and renowned gilding. In the large photo (left), a craftsman works to restore the original plasterwork in the Grand Ballroom, part of the Herculean $65 million restoration effort that began in 1982. In the inset photo, original plasterwork once again greets guests entering the Promenade. The gods of food and drink, Roman dieties Ceres and Bacchus (or as the Greeks called them Demeter and Dionysus) recline at the entrance to the dining area to indicate the abundant table that awaits. The accompanying cupids announce the abundance and serve up the fare the gods have bestowed. Restoration photo by Walter Smalling Jr., courtesy of Jessie Smail; detail photo by the author.

The restoration that would once again unmask many of The Mayflower's architectural assets would also uncover buried treasure lost for decades, such as those pictured here in the early 1930s with hotel silversmith Fred Glein (bottom). Workers discovered packed away in a long-locked basement storeroom valuable gold, silver and cloisonné serving and centerpieces, urns, vases and candelabra worth several thousand dollars each. Some of the silver remains in service; other pieces were put on display or once again relegated to storerooms. Gary Reidinger, director of engineering, stands in a storage area in the basement stacked from floor to ceiling with old silver service, urns, candelabra, and other reminders of the hotel's early opulence (inset). Propped on its side is a plaque formerly on display in the Promenade in honor of Mayflower staff members who volunteered for service in World War II. Reidinger photo by the author.

By now absent the more elegant Austrian carpets, the lush palms, the more lavishly upholstered gilt sofas and original urns and statuary, the lobby was like a lady without her jewels in this circa 1940 photo. Photo courtesy of Frank Fleming.

1984

A festive parade down Connecticut Avenue December 7th celebrates the completion of restoration and reopening of the celebrated Mayflower lobby.

By the mid-1960s and 1970s, the hotel had lost some of its glimmer and awnings darkened the entrances, foreshadowing darker days for The Mayflower. Cutouts below the windows accommodate individually controlled window air conditioning units which replaced central air conditioning. Color televisions replaced the black and whites and the spigot for running ice water was replaced by ice and soda machines on each floor. The improvements were part of the Westin renovation. Employees got a chance to own Mayflower furniture before it became part of a giant public sale. Photo by Youngsphoto, courtesy of Jessie Smail.

From Palm Court to Café

The history of the space that is now known as the Café Promenade is a time capsule of both the hotel and the nation. Named the Palm Court when it opened in 1925, it was originally a tea room featuring daily tea dances, or "tea dansants," directed by a Madame Mishtowt, wife of a former naval attaché of the Russian Embassy. In 1934, just months after the repeal of Prohibition in 1933, the Palm Court was renovated and renamed the Mayflower Lounge.

The increasing tension in Europe in the mid-1930s brought the most brilliant U.S. and allied military minds to the nation's capital, minds like Generals Marshall and Patton, and Admirals Mountbatten and Nimitz. Night after night during this time—and well beyond the end of World War II—the Mayflower Lounge was packed with top U.S. and allied government and military officials in high-level "chats" that raised the concern of Mayflower General Manager C. J. Mack regarding matters of national security. One casualty of the war was the beautiful skylight, which was blacked out and covered to conform to air-raid safety measures. It would stay covered and forgotten until forty years later.

For more than twenty years, The Mayflower had been a trendsetter, anticipating change and staying several steps ahead of the evolving needs of Washington society. But a misguided attempt in 1947 to modernize the Lounge not only cost the room some of its most renowned architectural details; it also cost The Mayflower its heretofore-loyal

The first official use of the Palm Court was the receiving line for dignitaries attending the inaugural ball for Calvin Coolidge. It became so popular that hundreds of Washington families introduced their teenage daughters to society at the debutante balls held there each year. In this 1930s photo, an elegant buffet awaits special guests in the Palm Court. Photo by Shutz.

customers. Designers removed much of the ornamental plaster work on the walls and ceilings, as well as the earthy color schemes, soft comfortable chairs, and soothing fountains, replacing them with grays and blacks, unupholstered chairs and stark walls. The "modernization" also walled off the French doors separating the room from the Promenade, thus taking away the openness for which both the Lounge and the earlier Palm Court had been known.

Described as "a space beautiful as the fabled hanging gardens of Babylon" when it opened in 1925, the Palm Court was like nothing seen before in the nation's capital. Gilded cages of singing canaries perched amidst growing vines, palms and blooming orchids. Latticed mirrors caught the light from the Palm Court's immense skylight, the largest in Washington at the time. As with the Café Promenade, its eventual successor, the Palm Court was completely open to the Promenade.

After the repeal of Prohibition, the transformation of the Palm Court to the Mayflower Lounge was inevitable. From its opening on Easter Monday afternoon in 1934, it quickly became the barometer for style, fashion and social standing in Washington, earning it the Washington Post's imprimatur as the "first stop on anyone's social itinerary." It was during the 1934 renovation that the room was closed off from the Promenade with French doors and windows.

It took management less than three years to realize their mistake and redo the room once again in 1949, this time eliminating the modern look in favor of a Georgian appearance. To extend the room's appeal, afternoon teas were once again added, to answer the needs of society ladies looking for a more refined way to spend their afternoons. Pat Nixon, wife of then-Vice President Richard M. Nixon, hosted a private tea in the Mayflower Lounge where the pastries were such a hit, she wrote a note to Chef Nicholas Marchitelli requesting the recipes. He respectfully declined to divulge his "secret" ingredients, but offered instead to prepare them for the Second Lady whenever, wherever and in as much quantity as she desired, according to a historical vignette on display in the Mayflower mezzanine.

By the late 1950s, the Mayflower's Town & Country and its "politically correct" Men's Bar were becoming so popular, it was decided that it was time to shift focus from the Lounge to full service dining. A new restaurant, The Presidential Dining Room, opened in 1957. Featuring dinner favorites of the past presidents, formal French service and Mr. Sidney's Mayflower Orchestra playing nightly, it was a hit from the outset. Reservations were a must. It was in the guest book at the main entrance of the dining room that former President Harry Truman signed his name followed by his occupation as "retired farmer."

Again, not content to let well enough alone, management directed another remodeling in 1967. Figuring that more was better, they went beyond even the elegance of the Presidential Dining Room with La Chatelaine, or "Mistress of the Castle." A historical diorama labeled it a "fantasyland of excesses," boasting "gargantuan candelabra, royal velvet chairs and couches suited for the most discriminating potentate," where "waiters in uniforms displaying more gold braid than a self-decorated head of state" served guests on crystal stemware, gold

The 1939 update to the Mayflower Lounge announced in this ad assured patrons that, aside from "new colorings, new draperies, new carpets . . . , nothing will be done to disturb the inviting atmosphere and rare warmth of the one and only Mayflower Lounge."

flatware, and gold-rimmed china, all amidst life-sized marble nymphs. A gong activated by a foot pedal announced the arrival of flaming offerings.

Though it survived only six years, it was routinely rated as one of the top restaurants in Washington. This was the sixties after all though, when all of "the establishment" was challenged by barefooted flower children flaunting free love. "La Chat" was labeled "too much." It was taken out of service as a restaurant and became a meeting room named the Presidential Room, the latest of several services to bear the name.

As with the leadership in Washington, the term "Presidential" reigned over several different eras at The Mayflower. At the opening in 1925, the first "Presidential Restaurant" faced the Promenade directly across from the original Palm Court. The Presidential name shifted across the Promenade to the Presidential Dining Room, which had replaced the Mayflower Lounge. It eventually devolved to merely a meeting room—the Presidential Room. Unlike the Palm Court–Mayflower Lounge, however, the original Presidential Restaurant underwent few changes except for the addition of a movable steel partition that divided it into the East and State Rooms where richly detailed gilt and polychrome state crests still line the walls. Sidney Seidenman Jr., son of the original Mr. Sidney who led the renowned Mayflower Orchestra for decades beginning in 1926, pointed out one other change on a recent tour of the rooms. At one end is a beautifully decorative metal railing at mezzanine height, the remnant of a now-enclosed balcony where Sidney Jr. played with musicians who entertained guests of the original Presidential Restaurant (now the East and State Rooms).

The transformation of the Palm Court–Mayflower Lounge in the early 1980s to the Café Promenade brought to light an art find: two large murals by prominent muralist Edward Laning and his assistant Philip A. Read. Although the murals had been in place for over a quarter-century, and the hotel believed them to be important works, their existence came as a surprise to the art world in general and even Laning scholars, who were virtually unaware of the murals' existence. Workers also rediscovered and restored the spectacular domed skylight that had been covered since the outbreak of World War II as part of The Mayflower's all-out civil defense effort.

Today, open once again to the Promenade, its murals uncovered, its skylight bouncing brilliant light off the restored chandelier and sconces, pieces of the hotel's original statuary at home once again, the Café Promenade provides a restrained re-creation of the ambiance that earned the original Palm Court such praise in 1925. Another feature also endures: luxurious tea and sumptuous pastries are still served every afternoon in The Mayflower, the first hotel in Washington to provide such amenities.

Notes Mayflower general manager George Cook Jr., "the Mediterranean cuisine, prepared by Chef Buggio, has proven extremely popular. The Café Promenade has become the hotel's premier restaurant and is a known power breakfast and lunch dining room. Dinners have the ambiance and the superb culinary presentations to rival any restaurant in Washington, D.C. This is quite a remarkable claim for any hotel restaurant and the Café Promenade proves itself every day."

In what was later termed an "ill-advised, poorly planned 'upgrading' project," The Mayflower's new managers under the Hilton chain took a stab at modernization in 1947. Gone was the warmth of the earthy color schemes, comfortable chairs, fountains, and general openness of the room. Instead of the airy French doors, a totally enclosed entrance opened now on somber grays and blacks, uncushioned chairs, and funereal draped walls. The change was a complete failure, both aesthetically and financially. Once-frequent guests made their feelings known immediately—they stopped coming. Only one feature of Hilton's ill-conceived modernization of the popular Mayflower Lounge in the late 1940s was mourned when The Lounge was restored to some of its former elegance: four murals depicting the Capitol, the Washington Monument, and the Lincoln and Jefferson Memorials by French artist Jean Pages were painted over. This rare photo depicting the Washington Monument mural is one of only a few that document the artwork, which survived for only three years.

It took only a bit more than two agonizing years for the Hilton management to realize the blunder they had made "modernizing" the Mayflower Lounge. Redecoration in 1949 ended the unofficial boycott and once again the Lounge became so popular that the amount of tippling there became a concern, especially in light of statistics showing that liquor consumption in Washington was three times higher than the nation's average. The Mayflower's teatime had been quite popular during the days of Coolidge and Hoover, when the Lounge was still the Palm Court, but the tradition had vanished since repeal of Prohibition. In 1950, none other than Mrs. Corneal Mack, wife of General Manager C. J. Mack, made a "valiant effort to sober up Washington a little," according to this Washington Post article announcing the reinstitution of afternoon tea in the Mayflower Lounge. Teetotalers paid $1 for tea accompanied by cinnamon toast, English muffins and cookies. A veteran of the cocktail circuit declared, "It won't work." Like many other less-than-sober predictions made in the Lounge over the years, however, this one also proved false. The Mayflower was the first hotel in Washington to serve tea daily; it remains one of its signature services.

Elise Morrow Says:

Tippling Washington Socialites Take Kindly to Tea at Lounge

WASHINGTON—The Mayflower Lounge, a spot hitherto devoted to fashionable capitalites who would rather be tight than president, started a revolution in Washington's social life this week. Promptly at 4 o'clock last Wednesday, and for two hours every succeeding afternoon, the customers started drinking tea instead of cocktails.

ELISE MORROW

This valiant effort to sober up Washington a little, roughly equivalent to enlisting Jack the Ripper in Gang Busters, was the brainchild of the Mayflower manager's wife, Mrs. Corneal Mack. So historic was the occasion that several of the capital's most prominent women gave tea parties to celebrate it, among them Mrs. Francis Matthews, wife of the Secretary of the Navy; Mrs. Owen Brewster, wife of the Senator from Maine; Mrs. Robert E. Lee, 3d, of the Robert E. Lees; Mrs. Harold Walker, a Washington grande dame; the Baroness von Schoen, Princess Christian of Hesse and Mrs. Lawrence Wood Robert.

Afternoon tea was quite a popular institution in the Coolidge and Hoover days when the Lounge was known as the Palm Court, but had all but vanished since repeal. Mrs. Mack got the idea of reviving the custom when she learned that, in recent months foreign diplomats were asking more and more frequently for tea. Now the hotel has set a standard price of $1 per person for tea with cinnamon toast, English muffins and cookies, and is going all-out to make tea drinking fashionable again.

"A quaint custom," one veteran of the cocktail circuit remarked. "It won't work," said another. Mrs. Mack was more hopeful but the Lounge was taking no chances—cocktails could still be purchased at tea time.

Washington is, as a matter of fact, getting just a little tired of the annual statistics on per capita liquor consumption. These invariably place the capital's sizzling rate three times higher than the nation's average.

The statistics are just as loaded as some of the people who contribute to them. Washington has a large and thirsty visiting fireman population, and many residents of nearby communities in Maryland and Virginia stock up on liquor in Washington. These factors distort the picture somewhat—Washington is not so think as you drunk it is. Nevertheless, the situation is appalling enough.

Another development on the sobriety front this week was the start of a series of broadcasts on "Alcoholism in Washington." This was sponsored by the Washington Committee for Education on Alcoholism and the local Department of Health.

Snacks and Beverages served in the atmosphere of an exclusive club for men . . .

NOON UNTIL 1 A. M.
ENTRANCE from MAIN LO[I]
AND CONNECTICUT AVE[N]

The MAYFLOWER
MEN'S BAR
WASHINGTON

By the late 1950s, The Mayflower's Town & Country Lounge and the Men's Bar, which opened in 1934 with 'patronage restricted to men,' had become extremely popular hangouts. So, in 1957, the Mayflower Lounge was transformed into a full service restaurant—the Presidential Dining Room. A hit from the outset, it featured the dinner favorites of the past presidents, formal French service, and Mr. Sidney's famed orchestra playing nightly.

Despite advice to strip them off, Kingdon Gould Jr., one of the owners of The Mayflower, decided to save the two "dirty, dusty and dulled murals" in the Café Promenade. Unknown even to the artist's wife, the signed artwork turned out to be the work of famed muralist Edward Laning and his assistant Philip S. Read. Laning is best known for his Works Project Administration murals of immigrants made for Ellis Island. Covered for almost half a century, the Italian Renaissance garden scenes, one of which is now featured on this contemporary Mayflower postcard, are framed with architectural elements to simulate vistas from columned verandahs.

La Chatelaine—"Mistress of the Castle"—replaced the Presidential Dining Room in 1967. A historical vignette on display today in the mezzanine states that the restaurant "thrived on the notion that more was better. . . . Waiters in uniforms displaying more gold braid than a self-decorated head of state served flaming kabobs of exotic meats from sabers the Three Musketeers would have been proud to wield. Gargantuan candelabra, royal velvet chairs and couches suited for the most discriminating potentate, crystal stemware, gold flatware, and agreeable life-sized marble nymphs surrounded you in the fantasyland of excesses." Strolling minstrels completed the tableau. Indeed it was more than the eye—or the camera—could capture at a glance, as seen in this photo from the period.

As if part of the statuary, a harpist in the Café Promenade serenades diners from her perch in the intimate oriel balcony. Shown here in the late 1980s, the Café Promenade was part of the first phase of renovations that began in 1982, a labor of love that returned The Mayflower to its former grandeur. Not only did the restorations uncover both the skylight blacked out during World War II and the Edward Laning murals, but it also reopened the area to the Promenade. Once again, art and architecture rivaling the greatest museums tastefully beckon guests not only to its elegant surroundings but also to four-star dining featuring continental American cuisine. Sadly, one piece of art shown here is no more. In the center alcove, just to the left of the torchiere, stands a large amphora made by French artist Louis-Joseph Grisee, 1822–1876, who studied at the Ecole des Beaux-Art. Just two years ago, a guest standing nearby knocked the piece to the marble floor where it shattered. Ever discreet Mayflower staff swept up the pieces and threw them away, not realizing that the valuable vase probably could have been restored. One of a pair, its mate, shown in the inset at left, now stands alone in another alcove to the right of the Café Promenade entrance. The pair had been appraised at $8,000 in 1980. Café Promenade photo courtesy of Frank Fleming; inset photo by the author.

The Good Ship Mayflower

One artist whose work still graces The Mayflower was James Gale Tyler. Born in New York in 1855, Tyler began painting at age fifteen. He gained local recognition almost immediately as a ship portraitist and by 1871, while still a teenager, he was studying with marine painter Archibald Cary Smith in New York City. Just ten years later, he exhibited at the National Academy of Design. It was about this time, approximately 1880, that his style became more impressionistic, broader and more romantic.

Just two of his works originally hung in the Promenade. The larger painting depicts the *Mayflower* landing, as Bradford described it in his journal. Recently restored, it has moved in the Promenade only so far as the wall opposite from its original location seventy-five years ago. In the second, smaller of the two Tyler paintings originally commissioned by the hotel, Tyler depicted the *Mayflower* off the New England coast with its sails full, its rigging covered with ice.

Early photos of the Promenade show only the one smaller painting, but it is now one of two that greet guests at the registration desk. Although it is uncertain when the second of the two smaller Tyler paintings came into The Mayflower's possession, it nevertheless provides the perfect match to its now-paired mate. In the second painting, the *Mayflower* sails into a spectacular sunset on seas still choppy after an apparent storm.

Director of Engineering Gary Reidinger discovered still a fourth *Mayflower* painting in 1999. While investigating the contents of the lower basement known as C2, he happened to notice a large painting, battered and covered with dust and crushed behind what once must have been an elegantly gilded but now equally battered credenza. He pulled the painting out into better light and could not believe his eyes. Although the canvas had at least twelve tears and was yellowed with age, it was

almost identical to the other large canvas depicting the *Mayflower* landing. On the left corner, it bore the distinctive signature, "James G. Tyler." Freshly repaired and restored, it now hangs beside the perpetually polished glass-and-brass front entrance.

While the cause for the painting's banishment is now lost, the story of its original acquisition is both clear and colorful. In a letter to Mayflower Manager C. J. Mack dated October 2, 1959, Captain C. Leslie Glenn, a chaplain and president of the Military Chaplains Association, wrote on official letterhead that the association had "an oil painting of the landing of the Pilgrims from the Mayflower. It is about 4′ by 6′— a good-sized picture and quite handsome, well framed, etc. We would like to give it to you." Captain Glenn went on to write:

"James G. Tyler, of Connecticut, celebrated marine artist, who with Mrs. Tyler, spent several weeks at The Mayflower in May" reads the caption under this picture of the artist in the June 1926 Log. Tyler was more than seventy at the time. The article stated that his visit *"served to call vividly to mind the important part which Mr. Tyler had in the initial embellishment of this hotel. Recognized as the premier marine artist of America and with many years of superb achievement in his chosen field of endeavor to his credit, this internationally known painter was chosen by* The Mayflower *management to execute the huge painting,* The Landing of the Mayflower, *which so handsomely decorates the walls of the Promenade and which, together with the painting of the Ship in action, which hangs between the elevators in the Main Lobby, has become the actual symbol of* The Mayflower *in the minds of all those visiting this hostelry."* The Log went on to note the success of sales of Tyler's work in America and England, *"and the picture selling best in England is the Constitution, the ship that gave that country the greatest worry during the war of 1812." Photo by Harris & Ewing.*

For many months in 1927, the cover of the Mayflower's Log *featured one of the two James G. Tyler paintings originally commissioned by the hotel. It depicts the ship with its rigging covered with ice shortly before its landing off the coast of Cape Cod November 19, 1620. By the time of a 1980 appraisal—which put its value at $3,000— it had been removed from the Promenade where it had hung beside a larger canvas depicting the ship's landing and was hanging in the general manager's office. Today, worth approximately $60,000, it is one of two Tyler* Mayflower *paintings that greet visitors at the registration desk. Photo by the author.*

"The painting is too overwhelming for the bedrooms in our chaplains' headquarters and it would be a shame to give it to the Salvation Army."

The Chaplains Association headquarters was only one block from the Mayflower, on 16th Street, so the charitable captain invited Mr. Mack to "just send someone up to the above address and the girls in the office will show it. At present, it is in the attic." Immediately Mr. Mack dispatched Resident Manager E. A. Eldred to see the painting and, less than a week after the chaplain's original letter, the painting was in the hands of its namesake hotel.

However at least one senior member of the association felt their president had overstepped his bounds. For the next year, letters flew back and forth with accusations between Captain Glenn and one Chaplain George F. Rixey, a brigadier general as well as the association's secretary-treasurer. In one letter to General Rixey, Glenn wrote, "Let me refresh your memory on the Mayflower painting. I gave it to Mr. Mack of the Mayflower Hotel because I thought it would be an appropriate place for it, and because I considered it a fire hazard in the attic . . . and it was certainly doing no one any good in storage. You said I had no right to do this and that the painting ought to have been sold instead. I had no hope of selling it. So I said if you could find a buyer I would give double what he offered

Although not one of the two original Tyler paintings owned by The Mayflower, this colorful depiction is the perfect match to the smaller original in both size and orientation. In it, the Mayflower *sails into a spectacular sunset on seas still choppy after an apparent storm. The breaking clouds reflect beautifully blended pastel pinks and yellows while most of the passengers appear to have come onboard deck after yet another of the "many fierce storms" William Bradford described that almost caused them to turn back. While unfurled after the storm and filled with the lingering wind, the sails still droop as if exhausted from the ship's battering. Photo by the author.*

This "large important Tyler painting," as described in a 1980 appraisal by Leland J. Arney, of Miller & Arney Antiques, Washington, was one of two present at the opening of The Mayflower in 1925. Signed by the artist on the lower right, it depicts the Pilgrims landing from the Mayflower. *John Alden, Priscilla Mullin, John Carver, Elder Brewster, and Myles Standish are pictured on the snow-and-ice covered beach with the ship anchored offshore in the background. In 1980, the painting was valued at $6,000; the 22k-gilded, hand-carved frame alone is now worth far more. Originally in the lobby, it now hangs in the Promenade amidst an array of stunning art. Photo by the author.*

and present the picture to Mr. Mack. You then went behind my back to Mr. Mack and asked him to buy what already had been given to him."

By July 1960 things had really gotten ugly. In another letter, this time on personal stationery, Glenn wrote to Mr. Mack, "I am delighted that you sent no $100 to that senile General. Just hang on to your picture and the $100."

However, though the battle was between the two chaplain-officers, Mr. Mack apparently thought surrender was in order. In a letter dated December 19, 1960, he enclosed a check for $100 "as a contribution to the Association in appreciation for the painting." But ten days later, in a handwritten note, Glenn wrote back, "I rescued your check out of the clutches of the Mil. Chap. Ass'n and destroyed it. So mark it cancelled. Happy New Year!"

Today even the frame alone is worth almost one hundred times what the hotel tried to pay. In fact, each of the frames in which the paintings now hang is worth as much as $10,000 by themselves. All four are intricately hand carved, and the frames of the first three paintings acquired by the hotel incorporate 22K gold paint in the finish. Of course the paintings themselves are worth many times more. The two smaller paintings have been appraised at approximately $60,000 each. The paintings, like the hotel they symbolize, have endured, complementing the grace and elegance that are the hallmarks of The Mayflower.

1985

The newly appointed People's Republic of China Ambassador to the United States, Han Xu, is guest of honor at a luncheon hosted by Stouffer Hotel President William N. Hulett. The Mayflower (under then-General Manager Hulett) had served as Han Xu's home thirteen years before when he brought the first delegation from China.

In this circa 1930 photo of the lobby, a Mayflower *replica* still stands on the table in the center. Another ghost ship, what appears to be a second Mayflower *model*, stands on the table just past the Promenade entrance in the left of the photo. The fate of one of these diminutive vessels is now lost; the other today greets guests at the concierge desk. The famous Puech statues are also barely visible down the length of the Promenade at far left. Photo by Blakeslee-Lane, courtesy of Frank Fleming.

This fourth Tyler painting of the Mayflower Landing was a hotly debated "gift" from the Military Chaplains Association in 1959. At some point it was banished to the hotel's basement. In 1999, it was found shoved behind an equally battered credenza; there were at least twelve tears in the canvas. Beautifully restored, it now hangs inside the front entrance of the hotel. At first glance, it appears to be almost an exact duplicate in size and subject to the hotel's original large painting of the landing that hangs to this day in the Promenade. However, closer examination reveals differences in several details: the ship itself faces in the opposite direction; at least six more settlers have come ashore to offload; and one workman or guard has set up a small cannon facing to sea. Photo by the author.

The Mayflower's Log

On March 1, 1925, *The Mayflower's Log* was launched. Scarcely two weeks earlier, on February 18, the hotel itself had come into existence. "A Monthly Chronicle of Mayflower Happenings," as stated on the cover of an early issue, for the next fifty years it eloquently captured in words and pictures every president and world leader, every entertainer, actor and artist, all Mayflower guests who would rise to world prominence or fall to disgrace during that span. It predicted both elections and fashions while showcasing the hotel's preeminence and renown as a stage for world events. Its official photographers included such talents as Underwood & Underwood and Harris & Ewing.

Published usually once a month, it contained as many as fifty pages of stories, poems, even ads for the best competing local as well as regional establishments, plus the current doings in the Washington scene, all for the price of a quarter. In 1940, it boasted "approximately three hundred and fifty readers a day . . . or ten thousand a month."

Covers from the *Log*, such as those shown here, depicted current events, original art, and contemporary photos of downtown D.C. The *Log* was discontinued under Hilton's ownership and, while it would be resurrected some years later, it never again achieved the size, scope and readership of its early days. Reviewed today, every surviving issue is a priceless reference of information and photos of early twentieth century world history and social affairs.

My Birthday

The Mayflower's Log—March 1, 1925

"A modest Magazine am I,
Prim, demure, and oh! so shy;
Really, hardly knowing how
Before the world to make my bow—
Yet eager for you, I confess,
To compliment my new spring dress.
Isn't it pretty?   Orange–blue,
Trim of line, all fluffy —new;
Nifty, jaunty, full of style,
Yet Puritanical the while.
Fetching, it is, I think,—don't you?
I'm pleased to death—hope you are, too.
With smile and bow and a 'how d'ye do,'
I here and now make my debut."

The Mayflower's Log—March 1, 1926

" Not so modest, now, am I—
Neither shy nor shrinking;
Chest puffed out and head held high,
I've won my spurs, I'm thinking.
Born one year ago today,
Crawling first, then toddling—
Now on sturdy legs I play,
Free from baby coddling.

"A traveled youngster, too, am I,—
North, east, south, west I've wandered;
On ships I sail, in the air I fly—
A fortune in stamps I've squandered.
But all the time I'm making friends,
Strong ties I'm busy binding;
A charm to life, I'll say, this lends,—
Success is sweet, I'm finding.

"So light the candle,—cut the cake,—
Your welcome will be hearty—
Come one, come all, and help me make
A happy birthday party!"

This poetic tribute to the hotel's auspicious beginning
and first anniversary appeared in the March 1, 1926,
issue of The Mayflower's Log.

Miraculously intact after seventy-five years, stone quoins still adorn the corners of The Mayflower's buff brick, and the French appliqué of classical urns, carved cornucopias, wreaths, and swags that adorn the façade retain their elegant details. The awnings pictured here are forever gone, replaced by adornments that enhance the original grand arches.

CHAPTER 6

Into a Century
More Beautiful with Time

*"After they had enjoyed fair winds and weather for a season, . . .
many times. . . the ship was shrewdly shaken, and her upper
works made very leaky. But in examining of all opinions, the master
and others affirmed they knew the ship to be very strong."*

—Of Plimouth Plantation, *the journal of*
William Bradford, governor of Plymouth Colony

Only miracles, makeovers and determined management at times kept open The Mayflower's doors. Beginning with Walker's downfall, the hotel struggled through its early years as it stretched for profits that would put it in the black. The second annual financial report published January 27, 1927, describes a period in the city's history unimaginable today, predicting, "The summer months, of course, in Washington never will be profitable except under some unusual conditions, such as a war period."

The smaller Shoreham Hotel had closed its doors in 1926, but the Carlton Hotel had just opened. The 1927 Mayflower financial report was also cautiously optimistic: "Washington hotel men generally seem to feel that conditions at the present time are subnormal, and the continued improvement shown by the Mayflower is, therefore, gratifying."

Eking its way through the lean years of the Great Depression, Mayflower hotel stock soared as Washington became the nerve center of world events that would march the nation into the Second World War. Rooms became so scarce that the hotel had to reserve accommodations for only those travelers involved in the business of defense. The "unusual conditions, such as a war period" did indeed fill Washington's hotels and coffers, and postwar Washington would never again slumber through the sultry summer. The capital of what was now the world's greatest power beckoned both businessmen and world leaders. For The Mayflower, happy days—and years—were here at last.

The wave of good fortune and optimism the nation rode in the post–World War II years and through the 1950s came crashing down dramatically and at times most tragically in the riptide of events that

The misguided modernizations depicted in these two photos blocked out the skylight and boarded up the elegantly wrought mezzanine that had been two of the hotel's hallmarks. Without them, it looked like any hotel in America. (Behind the front desk is employee Frank Fleming, now a night auditor with more than forty years of hotel service.) Construction photo by Capitol Photo Service, front desk photo courtesy of Frank Fleming.

defined the decade that followed. Racial tensions continued to build, and a civil rights march led by Dr. Martin Luther King August 28, 1963, brought into sharp focus both civil rights abuses and growing mistrust of the nation's leaders in Washington. While a turning point in the fight for racial equality, the specter of thousands of angry people swarming the Mall left dignitaries and tourists less inclined to stay in the downtown district. In the aftermath of the assassination of President John F. Kennedy on November 22, 1963, the black-draped White House cast a shadow that reached not only neighbors like The Mayflower but also the nation. The racial violence in downtown D.C. following the death of Dr. Martin Luther King Jr. on April 4, 1968, made many visitors to the capital fearful of staying in the downtown area. Employee Anton Lamplot of Engineering remembers those times: "During the riots, the employees stayed at the hotel for one whole week. We ate and slept here. Day and night we guarded all the doors ourselves."

Mayflower stock plummeted once again. Both guests and investors feared that The Mayflower's once-prime location had become a liability. But even before the 1968 riots, four men with Washington roots and an enduring

1987

On September 16th, while hundreds of spectators line Connecticut Avenue, Nikolai Nikolski of Circus Vargas crosses a 50-foot tight wire strung between The Mayflower's twin towers to celebrate the first anniversary of his and his wife's defection from the Soviet Union.

faith that The Mayflower was still a good investment, formed the partnership of May-Wash Associates and spent a mere $14 million to purchase the hotel in 1966 from the Sonnabend Family. At the time, considering her condition, even that amount was considered a risky bet.

Two of the four partners had worked The Mayflower's "back of the house" as young men: Ulysses Auger was a busboy in the 1930s, and Dominic Antonelli had worked as a parking-lot attendant. A third partner, William Cohen, got his start as a trash collector whose route included The Mayflower. The fourth man, Kingdon Gould Jr., was descended from financier Jay Gould and was the only partner who, in his youth, according to author Judith Cohen, "entered and left The Mayflower by the front door." Unfortunately, William Cohen died in 1973 but his son Richard shouldered his father's dream.

Almost sixty years after The Mayflower opened, Allan Walker's choice of designers and location would prove his real legacy and her salvation. Her magnificent architecture remained intact, and, according to Richard Cohen, The Mayflower's prime location on Connecticut Avenue, halfway between the White House and Dupont Circle, still gave it a distinct advantage.

Unlike Hilton, they proceeded cautiously with plans for The Mayflower's future, rejecting a 1971 proposal to demolish the hotel portion and turn it into a shopping mall. Not until 1981 would they publicly announce their decision to proceed with a plan that would restore much of the authenticity for which The Mayflower had been famous. Believing her strengths would overcome the troubles she faced, her new owners made a commitment of faith and finance that would cost $65 million—almost six times what it cost to build—and last from 1982 to 1984.

Stated Bernard Awenenti, vice-president and general manager at the time, "We probably could have torn down the original building and built a new hotel at a lower cost and in less time." Instead, The Mayflower hotel began a new voyage, one that would, in the words of Awenenti, preserve and renew the "heritage of the proud property that reflects so brightly the elegance and style of the grand hotel era in which it was built." The extensive renovation not only returned The Mayflower to its original appearance and authenticity as one of the world's grandest hotels, the effort also earned the hotel a listing on the National Register of Historic Places in November 1983, a distinction that helps guarantee her continued preservation well into the next millennium.

Having achieved what was almost an impossible dream, some time after the completion of renovations and a formal reopening on November 20, 1984, the May-Wash partners sold the hotel to Stouffer Hotels and its parent corporation, the Nestlé Company, who would own as well as manage the property until 1993. New World Development (later C.T.F. Holdings) of Hong Kong, proudly added The Mayflower, clearly once again an asset, to its other luxury worldwide properties, including the entire Stouffer chain of hotels which they operated under the name Renaissance Hotels.

By 1997 The Mayflower was indeed hot property, one of the jewels in fierce bidding for the Renaissance Hotel Group. A February 19, 1997, article in the *Washington Post* announced Marriott International as the winner in a deal that "helps achieve Marriott's goal of adding 120,000 rooms by 2000." The Mayflower, with its 660 guest rooms, including 76 junior suites and 2 grand suites—the Presidential and the Mayflower—was a significant addition to Marriott's portfolio of brands, including Renaissance Hotels and Resorts, an upscale, full-service brand with a collection of more than eighty distinctive properties in

Pictured here are three of the former owners of The Mayflower who saved her from possible destruction and invested $65 million in restoration. They are Ulysses "Blackie" Auger, left; William Cohen, center, whose son Richard would take on his father's dream after the elder Cohen died; and Dominic Antonelli, far right. Absent is the fourth member of May-Wash Associates, Kingdon Gould Jr., the only one of the four who, as the son of Jay Gould, financier and ambassador to the Netherlands, was recognized at the front door. The man second from left is Lynn Himmelman, president and later chief executive officer of Western International Hotels, head of Westin Hotels and Resorts at the time of the photo. The fifth man, second from right, is unidentified. Photo by Reni Newsphoto Service.

Convention Services Director Jessie Smail slings the sledgehammer signaling the beginning of restoration. Jessie asserts, "The hotel is the best it's ever been in my 27 years. They're making it authentic again, restoring the pride in its history by restoring the original marble and the (Mayflower) paintings. People know what The Mayflower stands for. It is the most famous hotel in D.C." Born into the hotel business in Atlantic City, New Jersey, she became the first woman convention service manager in D.C. Jessie says of The Mayflower, "We all have a devotion to this hotel. You walk in the door, into the lobby, and it lifts your spirits. It's always been that way." Photo by Mattox, courtesy of Jessie Smail.

Chandelier restoration expert David Toran and his assistant, Marion Johnson, began work at 1 a.m. to assemble and rehang the last of the Promenade's six restored chandeliers just weeks before The Mayflower's seventy-fifth birthday gala. Photo by the author.

twenty-six countries. In the United States, The Mayflower joined such luminaries as the Parc 55 Hotel in San Francisco, the Renaissance Beverly Hills, and the Renaissance Vinoy in St. Petersburg, Florida.

Now under the Marriott umbrella, Henry K. S. Cheng, chairman of the Renaissance Hotel Group and managing director of New World Development, stated in the *Washington Post* article that Marriott has the "experts to upgrade our hotels much better than we did. We strongly believe," he continued, "that under their leadership our property portfolio will be performing much, much better," he continued.

He was right. Under Marriott management The Mayflower continues to flourish. Capital improvements continue to keep her competitive, both cosmetically and structurally. The plumbing, electrical wiring, kitchens and renowned air conditioning systems have all been replaced with modern equipment. While The Mayflower may have been the first to offer "air-cooling," only recently did it

upgrade the inefficient boilers that had been in place since the 1925 opening. Gary Reidinger, Director of Engineering, states, "We just concluded conversion about one year ago." New boilers replaced the monstrous coal-burning system. As Reidinger conducted a tour of the new plant, Henry Talley, now assistant chief engineer, quietly went about his daily routine, checking all systems as they provide heat, cooling and hot water to the enormous kitchens as well as guest rooms of the now up-to-date hotel. Another longtime veteran of The Mayflower, Talley used to shovel coal to the old boilers, where the heat was almost unbearable.

Although the kitchens have been modernized, some things are better left unchanged. States Chef Norman Wade, "The stock pots are cooking all the time to make the gravies and the sauces. Most hotels now have their meats delivered, but we still have our own butcher. And the pastry chef still prepares the pastries right here."

Not since the first decade of its existence has The

Mayflower appeared so opulent and elegant. Renovations in the late 1990s required more than 56 miles of millwork in crown moldings; some 46,000 square feet of Italian marble were hand set in the baths. After ten years of painstaking effort by chandelier restoration expert David Toran, at $6,000 apiece, the last of the Promenade's main chandeliers was restored and rehung just weeks before The Mayflower's seventy-fifth birthday gala. And the last of four James Tyler paintings has been restored and now hangs at the entrance, joining those behind the registration desk and in the Promenade.

Marriott's commitment to preservation is evident. George Cook, general manager since 1999, is perhaps The Mayflower's most vocal champion for staying with the hotel's authenticity. "You look at the pictures of the hotel when it opened. Here's the lobby on day one and here's the lobby now. It's the same thing," he states. He intends to keep it that way. "When we negotiated with Thomas Pink out of London, Scotland and New York to lease one of the spaces in the front for a retail space, they wanted to consider redoing the front of the hotel a little bit, widening an outside door and making it like their New York store," Cook relates. During early negotiations, he had not yet let them know that "I wasn't going to let anyone touch this. Not as long as I'm general manager," he swore to himself. "So I took the architect outside and we walked to the middle of Connecticut Avenue on rush hour one morning and I said, 'Now look back at this building. Imagine 1925 and Model-Ts driving by. What you see before you is a masterpiece. It has not been changed for 75 years. We are not going to cut a hole in the marble unless it was there in the beginning. It's not going to happen. And if this is a deal breaker, so be it.'" It was not, and Thomas Pink, world-renowned men's clothiers, opened in August 2000. Ironically, further research revealed Thomas Pink's plans returned the Connecticut Street entrance more

Valerie Harper graciously pauses for a photo opportunity with Chet Whistler, Mayflower Evening Manager, in 1989.

closely to its original appearance. With approval from the Historic Preservation Trust, the doors were modified, and the clothiers have settled in for a fifteen-year lease.

In February 1999, The Mayflower's location would once again thrust her into the world spotlight. For ten days the hotel was under siege as twenty-seven satellite trucks parked outside to capture highlights from the House interview and, one week later, the Senate deposition of Monica Lewinsky in the hotel's Presidential Suite. The deposition was part of the impeachment proceedings of President William Jefferson Clinton.

In spite of all the media focus, the hotel still had other events and guests to serve. Manager George Cook tells this tale. The night after the deposition, prior to a match with the Washington Capitals, the New York Rangers were staying at the hotel. Hockey great Wayne Gretzky had played in the National Hockey League's all-star game in Atlanta the night before, where he had once again won most valuable player. Arriving separately from the rest of the team, his limousine pulled up to the front of the hotel where all cameras were aimed at whoever approached, ready to capture any glimpse of the infamous intern. In contrast, the appearance by Gretzky, arguably the greatest hockey player of all time, was anticlimactic. As he stepped out of the limousine, not a single camera flashed. The next morning he related to George Cook that it was the first time in his career that he walked by fifty photographers and not one person had taken a picture, to which a photographer replied, "Well Wayne, you're not the story."

While the impeachment proceedings were unusual for the nation, it is just that kind of history-making event that fires Cook's passion for The Mayflower and her guests. "Some hotels have a celebrity or two. Some have one or two a month, or three or four a month. Here it is a daily event. There was a

1988

The Mayflower's public restrooms are given a "3-seat" award as the best in Washington by the *Washington Post*, extending a tradition begun with its opening in 1925 when coin locks in the hotel's public toilets earned $421 for the year.

Mayflower General Manager Bernard Awenenti greets Chinese head of state Li Xiannian upon his arrival at The Mayflower in 1985.

morning two days after Saint Patrick's Day (1999) and I was in the lobby about quarter to nine. I was talking to [former U.S. Senator] Patricia Schroeder from Colorado, who had a group in the hotel. I turn around and [Wall Street investor] Michael Milken walks off the elevator. He was a guest here. I said 'Excuse me, Ms. Schroeder, I want to say hello to Mr. Milken.' I say 'Good morning, Mr. Milken. What brings you to our hotel?' and he said, 'Well I'm having breakfast with this gentleman.' So in the front door walks Jesse Jackson. They go sit to have breakfast. And after they're seated in the Café Promenade, I walk down the hall because Bertie Ahern, the prime minister of Ireland, is leaving. He was here for a St. Patrick's Day celebration at the White House. So we put him and Mrs. Ahern in the limousine. I turn from that and I walk back to the East Room and welcome First Lady Hillary Clinton who is speaking to a publisher's convention. It's now 9:45. All this in just one hour."

After fifteen years Bell Captain Joseph Brackeen still smiles when recalling that even the stars are human after all. He remembers Kurt Russell coming down from his room through the lobby wearing a ball cap one day. Russell and his son went to catch a cab, states Brackeen, but Russell thought the cab driver might be taking advantage of him and called Brackeen over for a consultation. "The $13 fare turned out to be about $7 too much," asserted Brackeen. Gene Wilder has also earned Brackeen's respect for his unassuming ways. "Mr. Wilder and his family travel by bus and train, so they take the subway from here to Union Station when they stay here." And Brackeen describes musician Barry Manilow as "just a real nice man."

Ellen Burstyn's colorful ensemble eclipses the more somber business elegance of Sandy Lavery (center), Mayflower Director of Sales, and Catherine Mrowiec, Sales and Marketing, in this 1989 photo.

"Visitors from across the seven seas, and home folk alike, find in this super-establishment rest and recreation," Beresford wrote in 1925. While it is the VIP guests who draw the public eye, The Mayflower staff realizes that its greatest success lies in its repeat customers. At an approximate 80 percent occupancy rate per year, some 300,000 guests stay annually, each one special to The Mayflower. It may be years, even decades before they return, but most usually do. One such couple—Laurie and Dwight Waynick—returned after fifty years. Now living in Greensboro, North Carolina, Mrs. Waynick wrote in a letter to Mayflower management dated May 14, 1999:

We were married on Saturday, October 22, [1949] and went to Washington and the Mayflower on our Honeymoon. We spent October 24th and 25th there. I have kept all of my memorabilia from that trip in my Wedding Book. You might find it interesting that our total bill was for $23.61. Each night's lodging cost $9.00 but we did have some additional charges for using the telephone and for the luxury of having a radio at the cost of $.50 a day. We also had a very 'big' amount of $3.75 for using a valet. I have the letter sent by Mr. J. P. Flanagan, Office Manager, to confirm our room reservations. I also have the complimentary bar of face soap supplied by the Hotel, and a Teletype Message which was sent to us while at the Hotel, postcards, and a piece of stationary [sic] showing the Mayflower logo. . . . As of this

Actress Veronica Hamill greets Mayflower Director of Security, Carl Crawford, during an event in the late 1980s.

Mr. and Mrs. Leonard Nimoy were also guests for a 1989 event.

Betty Friedan, left, renowned author of Feminine Mystique, *greets Sandy Lavery, The Mayflower's Director of Sales, in 1989.*

date, we are still happily married to each other and are looking forward to our 50th Anniversary.

The letter concluded with the couple's plans to retrace their honeymoon trip of half a century before, through the Virginia mountains to the Washington area, and requested information on accommodations at today's Mayflower. Jane Vorwig, executive assistant to Mr. Cook, brought "this special couple" to his attention. In his letter of response to the Waynicks, Cook wrote, "I'm certainly glad the hotel got your marriage off to such a good start," and invited them back for a complimentary two-night stay, including dinner and breakfast in the Café Promenade. In October 1999, almost fifty years to the day after their marriage, they returned to celebrate their anniversary.

While the Waynicks kept only soap and stationery, other guests over the years wanted more hefty mementos. One widow wrote to say that her husband had just passed away and she had always been upset that he had taken the hangars from The Mayflower during their stay there in the 1950s. In the package with her letter were the hangars.

Another pair of honeymooners made off with the silver coffee pot and sugar holder as their Mayflower souvenirs. That must have been the only "criminal" act in their lifetimes, however. After their deaths, their children returned the pieces, writing that for the past fifty-five years the coffee pot and sugar bowl had been sitting on the mantle in their house. Their presence always bothered the children, they wrote, "because our parents always taught us not to take things that didn't belong to us." Since the parents had now passed on, they wanted to return the silver to the rightful owner, The Mayflower.

Some write, not out of guilt but of gratitude. Wrote Thomas Pittard of Durham, North Carolina, "My wife and I were guests on the weekend of October 2nd. We chose The Mayflower because my family had stayed there 30 years ago in a sight-seeing trip and I remembered that I was in awe of the hotel. Since that time I have spent quite a bit of time traveling. I have had the opportunity to stay at hotels across the US and throughout Europe. Without any reservations, I can say that our stay with you was the best we have experienced."

Organizers of the American Academy of Ophthalmology's second Mayflower forum wrote: "Holding a conference over the dates of NATO's 50th Anniversary is something I'm not sure any meeting professional would look forward to but I must admit the Academy was always made to feel it was shown the same attention and flexibility to our needs. George [Cook] always stood ground in the Promenade to make sure both the Academy and the NATO officials were well taken care of. Never was the Academy made to feel like a second fiddle!" Of that same week in April 1999, the Honorable Jerzy Kozminski, ambassador of the Republic of Poland, would write, "On behalf of the Polish delegation to the Summit, it is my privilege to convey to you our sincere gratitude for your kind cooperation in assisting us with all the arrangements and the program. Thanks to your support we have managed to make the NATO's 50th Anniversary Summit a truly successful one."

Neither are momentous moments the special province of only the rich and famous. Remembers one woman, "The first time I went to tea with my grandmother and was allowed to wear stockings and white gloves, we came to The Mayflower." A camerawoman from NBC, at the hotel to cover a special event, confided, "I had my school prom here."

1991

Mayflower associate Octavia Spearman celebrates fifty years of service.

Talented jazz and classical musician Wynton Marsalis and his band perform for students of both Stevens and Thomson Elementary Schools, The Mayflower's adopted schools, December 1, 1993. Marsalis also taught the children the history of jazz and answered questions.

Hundreds, perhaps thousands, of couples have celebrated their weddings in grand style at The Mayflower. The tradition endures. Wrote Barbara and James Korman of their daughter's Fourth of July wedding, "Our daughter, Kathy, is the third generation of Kormans to be married at The Mayflower. She is our only child and we wanted the wedding to be perfect. Ms. [Lauren] Sandler . . . engendered our trust in The Mayflower organization. We were thrilled with the results. We were doubly pleased at the excellent service since we're Marriott shareholders."

These stories mean as much to the hotel staff as its promenade of stars. "So many testimonials—that's what a hotel of this stature earns, because people have made their own history at The Mayflower," Cook points out. Even after thirty years in hotel management, Cook's enthusiasm about The Mayflower is almost childlike. He confided, "This is my fourteenth hotel and I've never been associated with one

1994

On numerous occasions, Aldrich H. Ames, next to Benedict Arnold the most infamous traitor-spy in U.S. history, meets with Soviet officials at The Mayflower, one block from the Soviet Embassy.

quite like The Mayflower. I am absolutely honored to be part of this. We've got a living, breathing historical event taking place at this hotel almost all the time and that's exciting. That is the beauty of this hotel. Most of the players on the world stage stay here. And if you stay here, you're part of the history that is going to take place that day or that week."

The Mayflower's listing in on the National Register of Historic Places recognized not only its architectural significance but also its historic prominence as a place where famous public figures have lived and entertained. But like the hundreds of other historic sites in the Nation's capital, The Mayflower welcomes all visitors with the same level of service and undivided attention, for in today's rapidly changing society, service is as much a concern at the beginning of the twenty-first century as it was in the beginning of the last. As stated so prophetically in the May 1927 *Log*: "The flood of visitors from all over the world who annually pour into this city, hundreds of thousands strong, has necessitated hotel accommodations out of all proportion to the size of the city itself, and the ability of Washington to house huge throngs is unquestioned."

It has been said that the days of grand hotels as the

social centers of Washington are over. Those attending a recent Mayflower event would disagree. On March 23, 2000, Washington's grande dame celebrated her seventy-fifth birthday with a black-tie ball befitting her regal standing. As many as seven hundred guests filled the Grand Ballroom and other public spaces flung open in welcome and overflowing with flowers and food, from patés and puff pastries, chocolates and coffee liqueurs, to, of course, caviar and champagne, for toasting the anniversary. Among the countless dignitaries were such notables as Ambassador and Mrs. John Ernest Leigh, Republic of Sierra Leone, and Sir Courtney N. Blackman, ambassador from Barbados, and his wife Gloria.

Responding to the needs of their guests, institutions such as The Mayflower have evolved from places to see and be seen to havens of retreat and discretion, where stars and heads of state can count on privacy rather than fanfare. One need only review the guest list for any recent month or year to see that The Mayflower is still building on its "fabulous past," still amassing "plenty of great memories and one helluva scrapbook" as described by the *Washington Post* the day after the seventy-fifth birthday

gala. States public relations executive Charlie Brotman in the article, "As a native Washingtonian, I've seen a lot of changes. I think the Mayflower will always be 'The Mayflower.' It's a powerful name. In my opinion, a hundred years from now, this place is going to be right here." His words echo those of Beresford written 75 years ago:

> *Today . . . there stands a great edifice of twentieth century construction—of marble and stone, of concrete and brick, materials produced by the very transmutations of that time whose inroads they are designed to resist, and in the hands of man reshaped to his varying uses. . . . It was but yesterday that on this same site a circle of convent walls sheltered a garden close where laughing children trooped in and out while stately sisters strolled, reverently murmuring their prayers or telling their rosaries. Today on that acreage eleven huge stories of concrete and steel stand up-reared above city thoroughfares where daily to its doors sweep an army of motor cars and a throng of people, in all the rush and turmoil of modern industrial life. Time is indeed the great transformer!*

It was perhaps no accident that visionary Allan E. Walker chose as the location for his grand hotel the site of the former convent, where the soil had been consecrated as a haven where weary souls could find rest and refuge, where quiet reflection and deliberation revealed answers to those who sought meaning to life's most important challenges. Similarly, for three-quarters of a century, The Mayflower has been not only a haven for tired travelers but also a stage for events that have changed not only lives but also history itself. It is not only a place to make history but also to absorb it, for the very walls echo with events, both recorded and unwritten, that have literally changed the course of human events.

Like the convent, whose order "was born out of human love, loss, and friendship, lived in a community where gentle concern for others prevails," a life of service also leads the dedicated Mayflower staff. Seventy-five years after opening, The Mayflower

Although not represented at this March 16, 1995 ceremony, The Mayflower was one of two hotels awarded the Hotel Association of Washington 1995 Gold Key Public Relations Award for Community Service. The award cited the hotel's Adopt-A-School Program, designed to provide diverse educational and cultural experiences to students in an effort to expose them to the hospitality industry. Pictured from left to right are Michel Ducamp, General Manager of the Watergate and First Vice Chairman of the Hotel Association; Brad Edwards, General Manager of the D.C. Renaissance Hotel (The Mayflower's sister facility and partner in the program); Bob Bracey, Principal of Thomson Elementary; and Washington Councilman Kevin Chavous. Throughout each year, The Mayflower sponsors and promotes activities that involve the students from Thomson in hotel-related activities, including an essay contest in 1994 titled, "Why I Want To Be General Manager For A Day." In his winning entry, Olumide A.E. Ojeifo, a sixth grade student, wrote: "The opportunity of being General Manager is a path destined for success and that's why it's such an interest to me. I consider my character as being responsible, insightful, creative, trustworthy, and shrewed (sic). A General Manager must be like this to compete with other hotel chains."

proudly flies her pennants as a Four-Star, Four-Diamond hotel, a flagship of the Renaissance Hotels and Resorts brand of luxury, still the consummate hostess of celebrities, presidents, foreign dignitaries, and all her special guests. Its guestrooms, suites and acres of public spaces are as elegantly appointed as ever. The words of Mayflower builder Allan Walker's own granddaughter Kay Butterfield, in a letter written just two weeks after the hotel's seventy-fifth anniversary celebration, may capture the success of the hotel most succinctly: "Delicious food, lovely surroundings, history, and a kindred spirit. What more could I want?"

The words printed in a 1925 brochure were both promise and prediction: "In The Mayflower discriminating visitors from all over the world may find beauty, comfort and enjoyment. Here, surrounded by the official, diplomatic and social life of America's Capital, they may well linger in perfect contentment." In 1994, almost seventy years later, architectural historian Christopher Weeks wrote: "(T)he

Mayflower is exactly what a bouncy, big-city, luxury hotel ought to be. . . . The rambling lobbies and hallways are just plain fun, with their Aubusson carpets, Chippendale chairs, mirrored columns, and piped-in Strauss waltzes."

The successful symbol of the *Mayflower* vessel as a testament to endurance remains. Wrote William Bradford in his journal of the *Mayflower* voyage, "These troubles being blown over, and now all being compact together in one ship, they put to sea again with a prosperous wind, which continued divers days together." Like her namesake, as The Mayflower hotel sails into a new millennium toward a century as hostess, she does so with a grace that is timeless and with a legend of continuous service that is unsurpassed. On the anniversary of The Mayflower's seventy-fifth year, her crew, in a labor of love, has shaken her sheets and caught a fair wind. She sails into a century more beautiful with time.

Chant of Welcome

Four be the things that we wish for you here:
Happiness, comfort, good friends and good cheer.

Four be the things that we hope you're without:
Harm, inconvenience, trouble and doubt.

Three be the things that we hope you attain:
Pleasure and profit and every good gain.

Three be the things for which we ever yearn:
Your coming, your stay here, and your return.

Osgood Roberts
Mayflower Poet Laureate
and Director of Publicity, 1932

President William Jefferson Clinton and First Lady Hillary Rodham Clinton arrive at The Mayflower for an event in August 1998. Photo by Larry S. Glenn, courtesy of Jessie Smail.

General Manager George Cook greets Vice-President Al Gore as he arrives via the De Sales Street entrance in January 1999. In 2000, the vice president would be at the center of the nation's closest, perhaps most controversial election in history. Official White House photo.

1995

President Clinton, in a speech
at The Mayflower September 7th,
assures Americans that "there are
no Russian missiles" pointed
at the United States, a statement
that continues to be debated
to this day.

*House Democratic Leader Richard Gephardt,
right, arrives for a Democratic Congressional
Campaign Committee reception August 2,
1999, featuring a concert by Tony Bennett.*

*Tony Bennett entertains guests
at the Democratic Leader's
Victory Fund Event at The
Mayflower August 2, 1999,
"Congressman Gephardt's
most successful fundraiser in
his 23 years in Congress,"
according to a letter signed by
Heather Nalitt, Democratic
Congressional Campaign
Committee director of events.
The letter commended the
efforts of Mayflower Catering
Manager Helene Wilder who,
at the last minute, had to
accommodate 700 instead of
the expected 500 guests,
including more than a dozen
members of Congress. Photo
by Keith Jewell, Photo-Op,
Inc.; courtesy of the
Democratic Congressional
Campaign Committee.*

*Monica Lewinsky leaves The Mayflower
where she stayed in the Presidential Suite
during her deposition to the investigations
conducted by Kenneth Starr. Photo by
Ed Swiatkowski.*

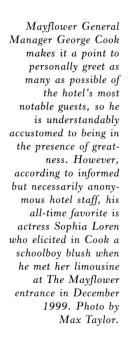

Mayflower General Manager George Cook makes it a point to personally greet as many as possible of the hotel's most notable guests, so he is understandably accustomed to being in the presence of greatness. However, according to informed but necessarily anonymous hotel staff, his all-time favorite is actress Sophia Loren who elicited in Cook a schoolboy blush when he met her limousine at The Mayflower entrance in December 1999. Photo by Max Taylor.

The Mayflower Brownies

Confectioners' sugar for dusting the pan and for topping the brownies

1¾ pounds semisweet chocolate

1½ pounds (6 sticks) unsalted butter, plus additional for greasing the pan

3 cups sugar

2 cups all-purpose flour

1 teaspoon salt

1 tablespoon baking powder

11 eggs

2 tablespoons vanilla extract

2 cups semisweet chocolate chips

2 cups chopped nuts (optional)

Dining manager Sunil Raikar handed out thick, chewy brownies from The Mayflower's own recipe to appease the hordes of reporters, photographers, lawyers, senators and members of Congress who descended on the historic Mayflower for the impeachment depositions in 1999.

Preheat oven to 350 degrees. Grease two 9-by-13-inch baking pans with butter and dust with confectioners' sugar.

In a saucepan or double boiler over low heat, melt the unsweetened chocolate and butter together. When chocolate has melted, take off the heat, stir to combine and let the mixture cool until just warm to the touch.

In the bowl of a standing mixer, combine the sugar, flour, salt and baking powder. Stir to mix thoroughly.

Add the eggs and vanilla to the cooled chocolate mixture, blending well. Pour this mixture into the bowl with the dry ingredients. Mix on medium speed for 30 seconds just until ingredients are blended. Stir in the chocolate chips and nuts, if using. Bake in preheated oven until the cake starts to come away from the sides of the pan, about 35 minutes. Cool and dust with confectioners' sugar before slicing. Makes 24 very large or 48 small brownies.

1997

National Football League owners convene at The Mayflower in October for two days of debate and discussion at their annual fall meeting; Vice-President Al Gore and First Lady Hillary Clinton address the January 22nd luncheon meeting of the National Abortion and Reproductive Rights Action League on the 24th anniversary of Roe v. Wade.

Right: Actor Jack Nicholson gets a personal escort through the lobby by General Manager Cook in December 1999.

For 38 years, student delegates to the William Randolph Hearst Foundation Senate Youth Program have come from all over the country for their annual meeting at The Mayflower. The Hearst family was there hosting one such event when they learned of the kidnapping of Patty Hearst on February 4, 1974. Pictured here are the 1999 Class of Delegates from the 37th Annual U.S. Senate Youth Program. In a handwritten note penned after his signature on an official letter of thanks to Jessie Smail, Thomas Eastham, Vice President and Western Director of the Hearst Foundation wrote, "Jessie—After 38 years it's like we all came over on the Mayflower." Photo courtesy of Jessie Smail.

Bill Russell makes his way through the lobby late one afternoon in 1999 for a stay at The Mayflower.

1998

Israeli Prime Minister Benjamin Netanyahu arrives at the hotel in January for Arab peace negotiations.

Attorney General Janet Reno addressed the Justice Department's National Symposium on Women Offenders held in the Mayflower ballroom December 15, 1999. Photo courtesy of the Department of Justice.

Above: Emily Lyons, left, the nurse severely injured in the 1998 Alabama abortion clinic bombing, was a guest of honor at the Planned Parenthood of Metropolitan Washington Champions of Choice Awards Luncheon October 5, 1999. Pictured with her in the lobby are Jatrice Martel Gaiter, center, president and chief executive officer of Planned Parenthood of Metropolitan Washington, and Carmen Urcia, Metropolitan Washington Planned Parenthood clinic manager. Keynote speaker was Kathleen Kennedy Townsend, Maryland's first woman lieutenant governor; Washington WJLA-TV news anchor Maureen Bunyan served as mistress of ceremonies. Photo by Theron Napoleon Whitaker, courtesy of Planned Parenthood of Metropolitan Washington, D.C.

Barry Hanrahan, assistant to the president of the Philadelphia Flyers, sent this team photo to Shannon Hadley, Mayflower Sales Manager, in appreciation for her impressive "ability to handle all last second changes that occur while hosting a professional sports team" during the team's stay in Washington as part of their 1999–2000 NHL season. Photo courtesy of Shannon Hadley.

The Parade Continues

General Manager George Cook Jr. has kept careful tally for his understandably proud mama of only those celebrities he has welcomed personally. Therefore, below is only a partial list of the luminaries who have graced The Mayflower since 1999.

LISTED ALPHABETICALLY

Bertie Ahern

Madeline Albright

Christiane Amanpour

Richard Armey

William "Billy" Baldwin

Ehud Barak

Bob Barker

Fred Barnes

Bob Barr

Marion Barry

Paul Begala

John Bennel

Tony Bennett

William Bennett

Paul Berry

David Bonior

Robert Bork

Sonia Braga

Donna Brazil

Ed Bryant

Maureen Bunyon

Chris Burry

Gary Busey

Jerzy Buzek

James Carville

Diego Cerrano

Plato Chacheris

Chevy Chase

Caesar Chavez

Henry Cisneros

Max Cleland

Hillary Clinton

William Clinton

Kathryn Crier

Walter Cronkite

David Crosby

Crown Prince of Thailand

Andrew Cuomo

Tom Daschle

Tom Davis

In a scene hauntingly similar to that of the photo of the Calvin Coolidge Charity Ball in 1925, guests crowd The Mayflower's Grand Ballroom for the seventy-fifth anniversary gala March 23, 2000.

On the first of a series of several events throughout its seventy-fifth anniversary in 2000, the hotel staged "Taxi Driver Appreciation Day" in February. Pausing from their duties that day handing out boxed lunches to taxi drivers are Mayflower General Manager George Cook, right, and, Crystal Christmas, Director of Marketing. The sign reads, "Thank you for helping us provide 75 years of excellent service to our guests."

Ambassador of the Republic of Sierra Leone, John Ernest Leigh, and his wife Elizabeth, both left, enjoy the hotel's seventy-fifth anniversary celebration with fellow Ambassador Sir Courtney N. Blackman, Barbados, and his wife Gloria, right. Photo by the author.

Right: General Manager George Cook and his wife Kathy toast The Mayflower's seventy-fifth anniversary. Photo by Mattox.

Director of Marketing Crystal Christmas gives a hug of thanks to seventy-fifth anniversary master of ceremonies and Washington celebrity, Paul Berry. Photo by Mattox.

Mike DeWine
Chris Dodd
Sam Donaldson
John Dye
Diane Feinstein
José Feliciano
Tom Foley
Steve Forbes
Al Franken
Dick Gephardt
Jack Germond
James Gilmore
Newt Gingrich
Parris Glendening
Dan Glickman
Danny Glover
Al Gore
Elizabeth "Tipper" Gore
Katharine Graham
Lindsay Graham
Phil Graham
Wayne Gretzky
Alexander Haig
Dennis Hastert
William Randolph Hearst
Charlton Heston
Eric Holder
Asa Hutchinson
Henry Hyde
Anthony Hopkins
Jesse Jackson
Carol Kane
David Kendall
Patrick Kennedy
Edward "Ted" Kennedy
Coretta Scott King
Henry Kissinger
Renée Knott
Morton Kondracke
Ted Koppel
Steve Largent
Frank Lautenberg
Patrick Leahy
Monica Lewinsky
Sophia Loren
Trent Lott
Emily Lyons
Joe Lieberman
Bill Marriott

Richard Masur

Kathleen Matthews

John McCain

Bill McCollum

Mary McAleese

George McGovern

Dee Dee Meyers

Michael Milken

Billy Mills

Donna Mills

Mrs. Mineyo Moscasio

Brian Mulroney

Jaques Nasser

Jack Nicholson

Al Neuharth

Oliver North

Tim O'Brien

Edward James Olmos

Dolly Parton

Jane Pauley

Simone Perez

Mary Kay Place

Abe Pollin

Carlo Ponti

Charles Rangel

Janet Reno

Bill Richardson

Richard Riley

Charles Robb

Cokie Roberts

Jay Rockefeller

Roy Roemer

Carl Rowan

Robert Rubin

Bill Russell

Tim Russert

Patricia Schroeder

Kerry Scruggs

Bernard Shaw

Eduard Shevardnadze

Nicole Seligman

Mr. & Mrs. Dennis Shepard

Ricky Skaggs

Jimmy Smits

Curt Smoke

Daniel Snyder

Donna Sommer

Arlen Specter

Jerry Springer

Jean Stapleton

While guests enjoyed the main buffet set up in the Grand Ballroom in honor of the seventy-fifth anniversary, a bounty of delicious desserts awaited them in the East and State Rooms. The menu offered delicacies reminiscent of the hotel's opening in 1925. Proud Mayflower staff await the genteel onslaught of the confections they so expertly prepared for guests at the gala. Pictured, left to right, are Marcos, José, Robert, Walter, Calvin, Lawrence, Gary Samson, Johnpa, Rafael, Janice, Myriam, Magali, Bobby, Cathy, and Michael. Photos by Mattox.

This contemporary watercolor by Washington artist Lonnie Jenkins hangs in the office of Mayflower Director of Engineering Gary Reidinger. Although a newcomer to The Mayflower, Reidinger quickly fell in love with The Mayflower madame and asked Jenkins, a close friend, if he would paint the picture from a snapshot. In many ways, however, the painting is as timeless as the hotel itself. Photo by Bob Ander.

Kenneth Starr

Mary Steenbergen

George Stephanopoulos

Connie Stevens

Helen Thomas

Fred Thompson

Victoria Tonseng

Nina Totenberg

Robert Torricelli

Kathleen Kennedy Townsend

Jesse Ventura

Lech Walesa

Dennis Weaver

Linda Wertheimer

Lynn Whitfield

Christie Todd Whitman

George Will

Stevie Wonder

Ronald Wyden

Neil Young

1999

Washington hosts NATO's 50th Anniversary Summit, an event that fills the district's streets as well as its hotels, including The Mayflower.

2000

For the first time since the communist nation was formed 55 years ago, a delegation from North Korea arrives in Washington to discuss normalized relations. Their home for the historic stay is The Mayflower.

The famous block-long Mayflower Promenade is once more polished to perfection.

Blocked up for decades, once again sunlight filters through the dramatic skylight and glimmers off the gilt capitals and other ornaments of The Mayflower, of which it was once said boasted more gold leaf than any other building in the country, except the Library of Congress. At night, fluorescent lamps cast a softer, evening glow of the glass panes, so it is never dark.

One of two original bronze figures extends outstretched arms in welcome to the Café Promenade. Its skylight gleaming, the Edward Laning murals beautifully restored, meals cooked to perfection, once again, as architect and hotel designer Robert Beresford wrote in 1925, the "luxuriousness of its appointments and the completeness of its service" appeal instantly to its guests.

The Grand Ballroom is once again the belle of Washington's balls, where kings and queens, presidents and prime ministers have dined and danced for three-quarters of a century.

The Chinese Room gleams like new, its domed ceiling elaborately distracting yet ready to surprise the next unsuspecting guest with its unique talent for broadcasting sound. Photo by Mattox.

Below: The Mayflower Suite comes complete with its own balcony, the only one in the hotel. Located on the third floor, it provides a panoramic view of Connecticut Avenue.

2001

During 2001 inaugural festivities, the Republican National Committee books a block of 350 rooms to accommodate such notables as Muhammad Ali, Peter Asher, Delta Burke and Gerald McRaney, Drew Carey, Dixie Carter, Nell Carter, Kelsey Grammer, Rudolph Giuliani, Marie Osmond, Sandi Patti, Pat Sajak, Rick Schroeder and Connie Stevens.

The parlor of the Presidential Suite is as elaborately
appointed as any mansion.

The entrance to
the Presidential
Suite, on the
third floor of the
hotel, boasts its
own skylight.

Lacking the ornate wood paneling of the Presidential Suite,
The Mayflower Suite is more light and airy and is more suited
to feminine tastes, such as those of guest Diane Sawyer, states
Tracy Harris, assistant to the director of marketing.

An elegantly wood-paneled concierge desk stands centrally located directly across the main elevators in The Mayflower lobby, where the multilingual staff provides every kind of assistance, regardless of nationality. It is also now the perfect place to spotlight the original Mayflower replica that continues to symbolize the hotel's endurance as a flagship hotel.

Select Bibliography

This bibliography is by no means a complete record of all the works and sources I have consulted. In addition to scores of interviews, it indicates the substance and range of reading upon which my information is based. I intend it as a convenience for those who wish to pursue the panoply of events that have played out on The Mayflower stage.

All photos and illustrations are from Mayflower archives, unless otherwise noted.

Books

Bruun, Erik, and Jay Crosby, ed. *Our Nation's Archive: The History of the United States in Documents*, New York: Black Dog & Leventhal Publishers, 1999.

Churchill, Winston S., ed. *The Great Republic: A History of America*, Random House, 1999.

Foner, Eric, and John A. Garraty, ed. *The Reader's Companion to American History*, Boston: Houghton Mifflin Company, 1991.

Gallagher, Patricia, ed., et al., *Washington, D.C.: a Smithsonian Book of the Nation's Capital*, Washington: Smithsonian Institution, 1992.

Grun, Bernard, *The Timetables of History: A Horizontal Linkage of People and Events*, New York: Simon and Schuster, 1982.

Long Island: Our Story, Melville, New York: Newsday, 1998.

New York Times: 100 Years of Headlines, New York: The New York Times Company, 2000.

Rosenblum, Constance, *Gold Digger: The Outrageous Life and Times of Peggy Hopkins Joyce*, New York : Metropolitan Books, 2000.

Scott, Pamela, and Antoinette J. Lee, *Buildings of the District of Columbia*, New York: Oxford University Press, 1993.

Simon, Philip J., *Log of the Mayflower*, Chicago: Priam Press, Inc., 1980.

Spinrad, Leonard, and Thelma Spinrad, *On This Day in History*, rev. by Anistatia R. Miller and Jared M. Brown, Prentice Hall, 1999.

Weeks, Christopher. *Guide to the Architecture of Washington, D.C.* 3rd ed. Baltimore and London: The Johns Hopkins University Press, 1994.

Newspapers

Daily News, 7 January–11 February 1985

Evening Star, 15 May 1925

Gaithersburg Gazette, 22 July 1998

Hotel Corporation of America News, April 1965

Hotel Gazette, 4 January, 1947

Hotel & Motel Management, March 1985

Il Progresso, 19 August 1936

Inn-side HCA, February 1969

InTowner, May 1996

Mayflower's Log, 1926 to 1981

Miami Herald, 20 March 1986

New York Times, 1 October 1959

Rudder, Mayflower magazine, June 1927

Staten Island Advance, 9 April 1975

Times-Dispatch, 19–22 January 1997

Washington Post, 1925–2001

Washington Times, 29 April 1985

Articles

Beresford, Robert F. "The Mayflower: Washington's Largest and Latest Hostelry," *Through the Ages*, ca. 1927.

Busch, Noel F. "Hilton the Host: A bold and agile Texan keeps adding new hotels to world's No. 1 chain." Publication unknown, ca. 1949.

Griffin, Barbara J. "The Life of a Poor Relation: The Art and Artistry of Marietta Minnigerode Andrews," *Virginia Cavalcade*, Spring 1991, Vol. 40, No. 4, pp. 148–159.

Griffin, Barbara J. "The Life of a Poor Relation: The Art and Artistry of Marietta Minnigerode Andrews," *Virginia Cavalcade*, Summer 1991, Vol. 41, No. 1, pp. 20–33.

International Steward, 1948.

"Profile of George DeKornfeld," *Impressions*, Spring, 1984.

Papers

Kansas City Public Library, Special Collections.

Maxwell, Shirley. National Register of Historic Places Inventory—Nomination Form, Mayflower Hotel, Alexandria, Va., Massey Maxwell Associates, 24 February 1983.

Mayflower Chronology, 1999, compiled by Frank Fleming.

Reports

Mayflower Hotel Corporation, Annual Reports, 1926–1940.

Collections

Biographical Dictionary, electronic resource for biographical information.

Heritage Preservation, Washington, D.C.

Historical Society of Washington, D.C.

Library of Congress.

Making of America Collection, Cornell University Library, Michigan.

National Women's Hall of Fame, Seneca Falls, New York.

Order of the Visitation of Holy Mary, Washington, D. C.

Political Graveyard, electronic resource for U.S. political history.

Index

About the Author

An avid reader since she was five, the writing bug bit Diana Bailey when she was twelve years old and her first essay was published in the local newspaper in Key West, Florida. She turned her passion for reading and words into her profession as an editor and journalist for more than twenty-five years. She has edited at least twenty pictorial histories, including *The Squares: An Introduction to Savannah; Diamond in the Rough: An Illustrated History of Arizona; Atlantic County: A Pictorial History; Cities on the Saco;* and *Wings of Valor, Wings of Gold,* an in-depth pictorial accounting of the lives of naval aviation pioneers. She also collaborated on the biography, *My First Seventy Years in Golf,* by international golf legend Chandler Harper.

As a journalist, Diana has had hundreds of articles published in national and regional magazines and newspapers, most recently as guest essayist for the *Virginian-Pilot,* the newspaper serving the metropolitan Hampton Roads area.

Several of her essays have also been broadcast on public radio in Richmond, Virginia, where she was a charter member of "Night Writers," a group of recovering writers under the stern but gifted tutelage of author and essayist Phyllis Theroux.

She lives on a lake in Virginia Beach with her husband Ken and her favorite canoeing companion, Jake.

Author Diana L. Bailey at home in Virginia.

THE P
TO